PRAIRIE PLANTS of ILLINOIS

*A Field Guide to the Wildflowers and
Prairie Grasses of Illinois and the Midwest*

STEVE W. CHADDE

"The sea, the woods, the mountains, all suffer in comparison with the prairie...the prairie has a stronger hold upon the senses. Its sublimity arises from its unbounded extent, and its still, unmoved, calm, stern, almost self-confident grandeur."
—Albert Pike, *Journeys in the Prairie, 1832*

PRAIRIE PLANTS OF ILLINOIS
A Field Guide to the Wildflowers and Prairie Grasses of Illinois and the Midwest

STEVE W. CHADDE

Copyright © 2019 by Steve W. Chadde
All rights reserved.
Printed in the United States of America.

This work is an updated and revised derivative of *Prairie Plants of Illinois* (1985) by John W. Voigt (Department of Botany, Southern Illinois University) and Robert H. Mohlenbrock (Department of Botany Southern Illinois University), with Illustrations by Miriam Mysong Meyer, in cooperation with the Illinois Department of Conservation, Division of Forest Resources and Natural Heritage. Available under a Creative Commons Attribution 4.0 licence (CC BY 4.0). For more information see: *https://creativecommons.org/licenses/by/4.0/*.

The Biota of North America Program (*www.bonap.org*) provided permission to use their data to generate the distribution maps.

AN ORCHARD INNOVATIONS BOOK
ISBN 978-1-951682-13-2

VERSION 1.0, 11/01/2019

CONTENTS

Introduction 5

Illustrated Glossary. 11

Glossary. 16

Key to the Groups of Prairie Plants 18

Prairie Plants—Descriptions and Illustrations 33

    Group A: All the leaves confined to the base of the plant; leaves not long and narrow, never ten times longer than broad. 33

    Group B: Leaves, or some of them, compound, that is, divided into 3 or more distinct segments or leaflets. 49

    Group C: Leaves simple, opposite or whorled. 93

    Group D: Leaves simple, alternate. 142

    Group E: Leaves long and narrow, at least ten times longer than broad; leaves with parallel veins; flowers showy, yellow, lavender, purple, blue, orange, or white. 213

    Group F: Leaves long and narrow, at least ten times longer than broad; leaves with parallel veins; flowers inconspicuous, green or brown or straw-colored, without petals. 237

Acknowledgments. 283

References. 284

Index to Common and Scientific Names. 285

COMMON PRAIRIE DOMINANTS

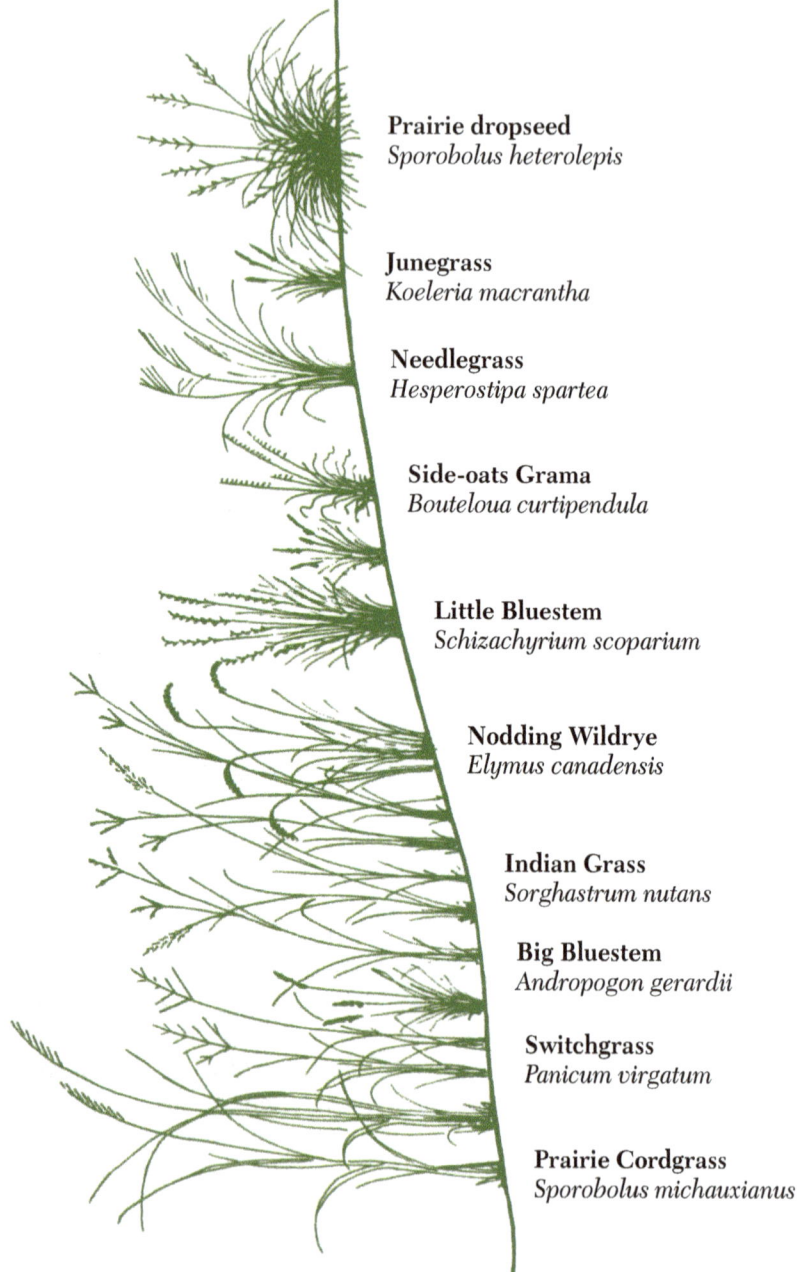

Fig. 1. Important dominant grasses of Illinois prairie along a moisture gradient from wet (bottom) to drier (top).

INTRODUCTION

This book is designed to provide a better understanding of the prairie plants which comprise a rich vegetational heritage in Illinois.

French explorers and trappers, upon viewing the extensive grasslands of mid-America for the first time, called them "Prairie." Their word had the meaning of a natural meadow. Prairie is a word related to the Latin "pratum", which means meadow.

Prairie is a vegetational community dominated by native grasses. Subordinate to the grasses are many colorful herbs that delight the eye of the traveler and the observer. Interesting patterns are also created by the rippling motion of the grasses under the wind, and shadows by the sun and clouds. The vastness of the land, its rolling topography, motion of the grasses, and changing light and shadows gave the illusion of the ground heaving and swelling and appealed to the same emotions as did the endless oceans.

The prairie was created over a period of thousands of years. Its species became adjusted to the reactions they made upon and among each other and to the extremes of continental climate. The species accommodated each other's needs by differences in stature and in seasonal appearance. The prairie flora became adjusted to grazing by herds of ungulates and to ravaging of wildfire when the plants were dry at maturity. All these factors and others combined to make the prairie a richly integrated community.

In many places the prairie flora will be found to be relatively simple. In Iowa, Shimek, who was an early student of prairie, found the flora to be composed of about 265 species. In Nebraska, on a square mile of prairie, Steiger found 237 species. More than 300 species were indigenous to the prairies of Illinois.

The student of prairie vegetation in Illinois will meet only about ten species of grasses with regularity. These ten species constitute the major dominants (Fig. 1). Several other secondary grass species are encountered much less frequently. About three dozen species of forbs will occur in regularity, and another fifty or more forbs will grow in lesser number and with lessened frequency. The remaining forb species are widely distributed, and even of less frequent occurrence. Some of them are classed as rare. A relatively few species make up most of the vegetation in some prairies, but in others, such as sand prairies, hill prairies, and savannas,

ILLINOIS PRAIRIE

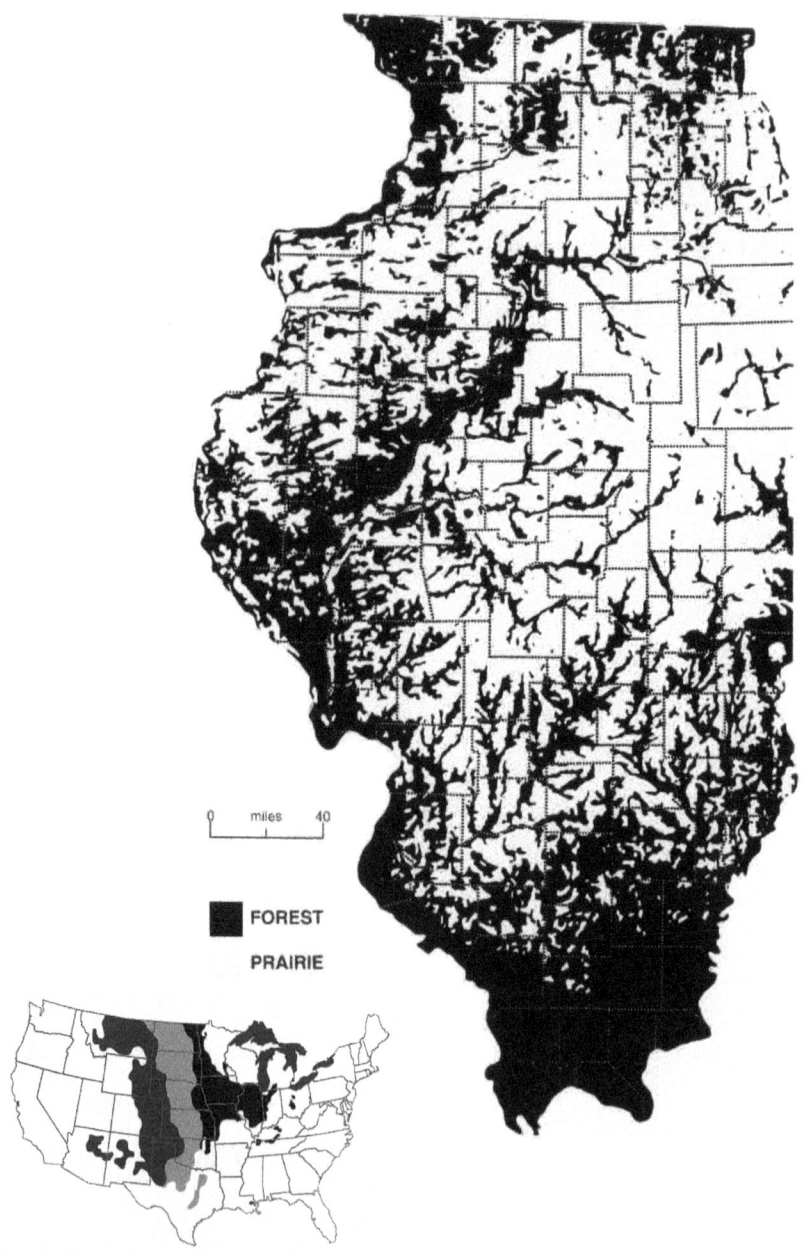

Fig. 2. Approximate extent of prairie and forest vegetation in presettlement Illinois. INSET. Original extent of prairie in the United States; tallgrass prairie shown in black, mixed-grass prairie in light gray; shortgrass prairie, dark gray.

INTRODUCTION

many additional species are encountered. By becoming acquainted with about fifty species, including both grasses and forbs, one has made a good beginning in the study of prairie. By increasing the number of familiar species to over one hundred, one feels at home in most prairie situations and has, by this time, learned the more important habitat associations and community relations among the dominants.

Throughout Illinois there were marked differences in the growth of plants. In addition to the obvious factor of climate, there were differences in drainage, soil quality, topography, degree of burning, kinds of animals present, as well as many other factors. When all of these became integrated, they expressed recognizable geographic variations in the appearance of prairie.

The prairies of Illinois were bounded on the east by the deciduous forest. Often there was a transition area of savanna, particularly in northeastern Illinois. Rainfall was an important factor upon the growth and stature of the prairie grasses. Our Illinois prairies were chiefly tall grasses and tall herbs intermingled with grasses and herbs of middle stature. There were, as well, some grasses and herbs of short stature. There is a gradient from short to tall grasses with the shorter plants blooming in the spring and the taller plants blooming in the fall. Our "tall grass prairies" had a three-layered structure; they were called the True Prairie (Fig. 2). True Prairie extended westward to a broad transition area near the 97th Meridian where it gave way to Mixed Prairie. Mixed Prairie was so named because it was a mixture of mid- and short grasses and herbs. The Mixed Prairie extended over 400 miles farther west to the Rocky Mountains, and ranged north from Canada and south to Texas and old Mexico.

Prairies of mid-continental America owe their existence to the geological uplifting of the Rocky Mountains millions of years ago. As a result of the mountain building, the westerly winds were caused to drop their moisture on the west slopes of the Rockies, creating a rain shadow on the east side of the mountains. This increased the dryness and speeded the evolution of the grass life form and of the spread of grassland vegetation over the plains area. Mammals, including a number of grazing types such as horses rhinoceros, and camels, evolved simultaneously and were present in North America in the Eocene epoch when the grasslands were developed.

About 200,000 years ago, glaciation destroyed most of the vegetation

INTRODUCTION

in what is now Illinois. Upon retreat of glacial ice, prairies became established upon the new lands. The deepest penetration of this glaciation was to within 50 or 60 miles of the southern tip of Illinois. A most recent glaciation, the Wisconsinan, occurred about 10,000 years ago, and covered the northeastern third of the state.

Illinois prairies as seen by the early French explorers were largely on the glaciated lands. Most of the present prairie remnants are also on glaciated lands. Exceptions are the small inclusions of prairie within the forests south of the glacial limits or on the bluffs and the driftless areas which escaped glaciation.

Scattered lowland areas developed following continental glaciation. There was a slow migration of prairie onto unglaciated lands. These areas were extensive in eastern and northeastern Illinois and supported wet prairie. There were also lowland areas not quite so wet which were simply lowland prairie. The upland prairies were drier and these were quickly put into agricultural use. The largest part of the great Illinois prairie was either upland or lowland-wet prairie types. Before settlement, about two-thirds of the vegetation in what is now the State of Illinois was native or natural grassland. Illinois became known at an early date as the "Prairie State."

Along the sides of the Rock River Valley of northern Illinois, there are deposits of glacial rock or gravel outwash. Upon these areas there developed a distinctive type of prairie which showed some affinities with the prairies to the West. This kind of prairie, dry because of porous gravel, is known as the Gravel Hill Prairie.

In other places, particularly along the Mississippi and Illinois Rivers, there were deposits of river sand where prairie vegetation developed. The largest of these is in the Illinois River valley in Mason and adjoining counties. These Sand Prairies show a strong affinity to the western prairies in terms of their species composition.

At the turn of the century, these prairies were studied by Dr. Henry Allan Gleason, famous American plant ecologist. One of the Nature Preserves in Illinois in Mason County is named in honor of Dr. Gleason, who was a native of Illinois.

As the ice sheet of the continental glacier receded, its melt waters created braided streams which covered broad valleys. This left exposed much fine-textured soil material which upon drying, was blown onto the

INTRODUCTION

uplands and deposited as loess. On these loess-covered hills, some prairies developed. The prairies bordering the major rivers were called Loess Hill Prairies.

The early prairie pioneers depended upon the prairie as a source of forage for their livestock. As the prairies were grazed by domestic stock, the vegetation began to change. Some species were more palatable and nutritious. These were constantly sought and grazed, and the plants were weakened and replaced by others. Thus, some plants decreased, some increased, and many introduced species became established as invaders. Over a period of time, the prairie lost its stability because its carrying capacity was exceeded. The original character of the prairie was changed by a replacement of native species by those of outside origin and of a weedy nature.

Native grasses continue to have many uses. They are important in erosion control, forage production, wildlife food and cover, reclamation, roadside planting, and beautification projects. Native grasses and grasslands have provided agricultural soils of unmatched richness. One needs only to look at maps showing the distribution and productivity of cereal grain or of farmland concentration to see the close correspondence the present cultural landscape and economy have with the original range of the bluestem grasses, the prairie chicken, the bison, and other native species of the prairies. Prairie grasses are an important part of our heritage and underlie our very existence.

There are many grassy places in nature today. Some are fescue pastures, Kentucky bluegrass lawns, and hay meadows containing various grass mixtures of foreign introductions. Such places contain almost wholly non-native species, and this separates them from prairie which is made up entirely of native grasses and herbs. A well-developed prairie makes no accommodation to foreign introductions. Only when prairie has been weakened does it allow entry of outside or foreign elements. Woody species seldom are present in prairie in any significant number, except at margins of prairie where the prairie contacts the forest, or up the ravines where added protection is given to woody species.

The quality of a prairie is proportional to the protection and care it has received. Once a good prairie has been seen and its composition and structure understood, then judging the quality of another is made easier. Excessive or uncontrolled use degrades a prairie. Grazing, herbiciding,

INTRODUCTION

mowing, plowing, drainage, and lack of fire affect all prairie species. Each kind of disturbance affects the prairie species somewhat differently. Each species has its own limits of tolerance to various factors. Some species are deep-rooted and have abundant food reserves; other species are unpalatable and escape grazing. Such species last longer in prairies than others. These remaining species are called relicts, and they give us clues as to what kind of vegetation once occupied the area.

The quality of a prairie is often judged by the native species which remain, although this is not always the case. One must get to know the native species. Look for a well developed structure such as layering, well marked communities, and well marked seasonal aspects. The dark soil of a former prairie or a relict prairie will reflect the occupation of the area by grasses. Conversely, a lack of any of these features, or the presence of bare soil, erosion, or the presence of annual or invading species among a few relict prairie species, often reflects a degenerated prairie.

In our rush to settle the land, only a few prairies and some remnants remain. Both the relict prairies, and the remnants which remain, are worthy of our best efforts to maintain, increase, study, and enjoy.

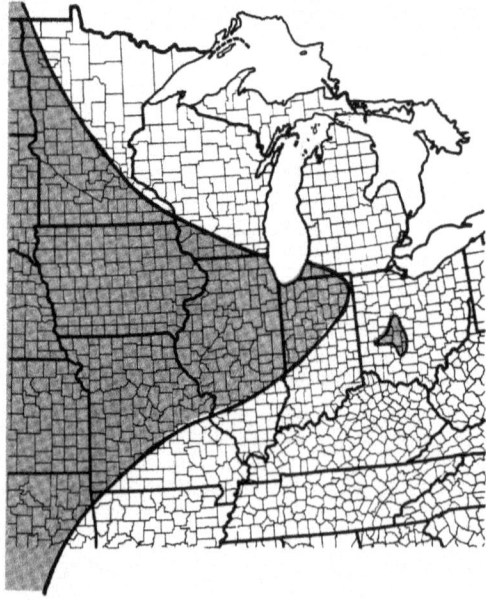

Shaded area indicates approximate extent of True Prairie in the Midwest.

ILLUSTRATED GLOSSARY

In order to distinguish one kind of prairie plant from another, it is necessary to learn the major characteristics which these prairie plants of Illinois may possess. Illustrated on the next few pages are several of the most commonly encountered characteristics of leaves, flowers, and their arrangement (Characters 1-4). A thorough understanding of these structures will insure a quicker and more accurate identification.

On the pages following the illustrated glossary and glossary are keys to the prairie plants of Illinois. A key is a botanical device which enables the user, through proper selection of a series of choices, to identify a specimen at hand. Begin with the first pair of number 1's, choose the statement that best fits the unknown specimen, and then go to the next correct pair of statements. Continue this procedure until the name of the plant is reached.

Prairie dominated by big bluestem (*Andropogon gerardii*) with sawtooth sunflower (*Helianthus grosseserratus*).

Character 1. LEAF CHARACTERISTICS

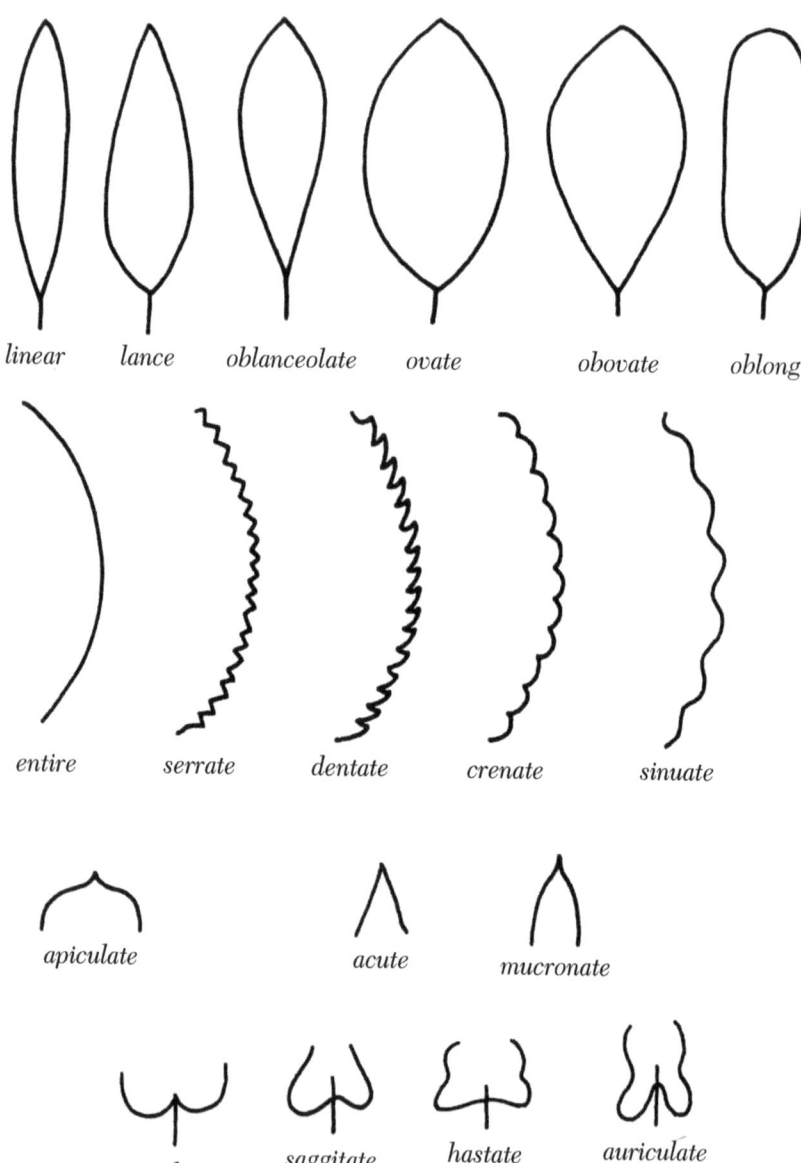

Character 2. LEAF ARRANGEMENTS

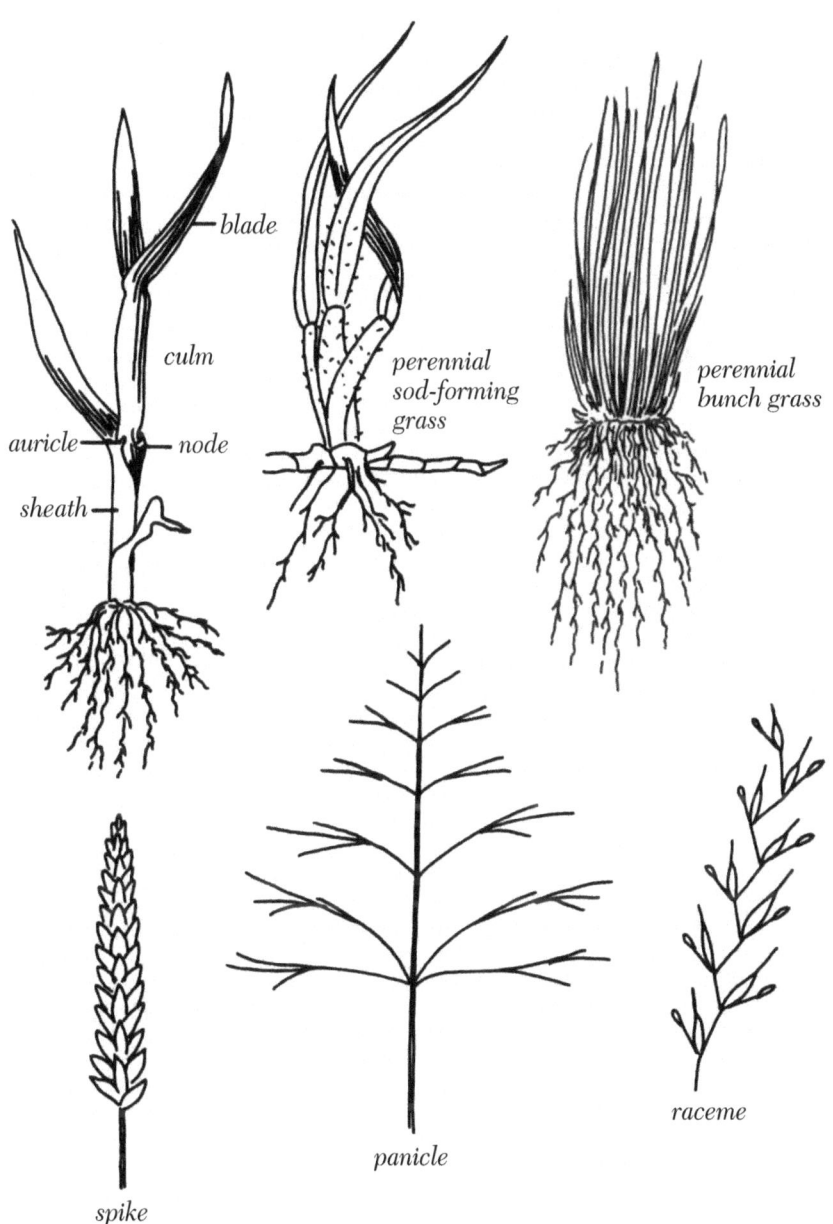

Character 3. FLOWER CHARACTERISTICS

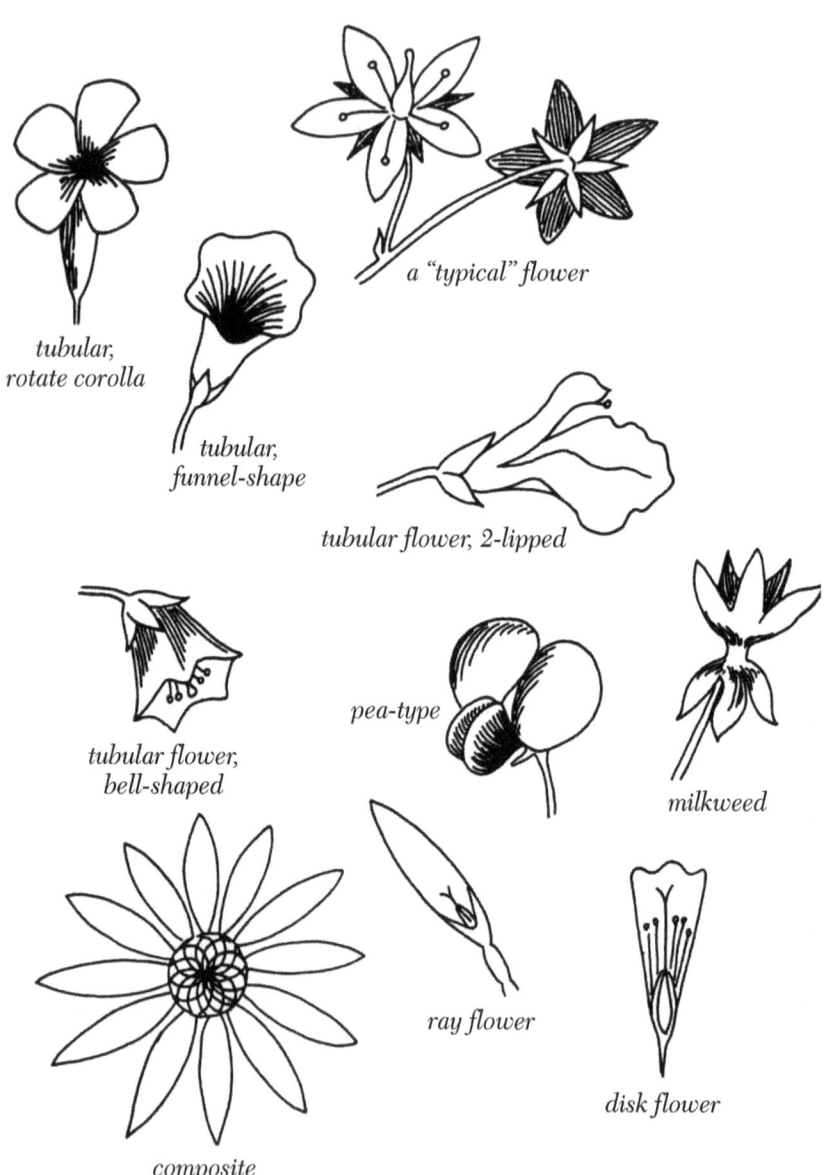

Character 4. FLOWER ARRANGEMENTS

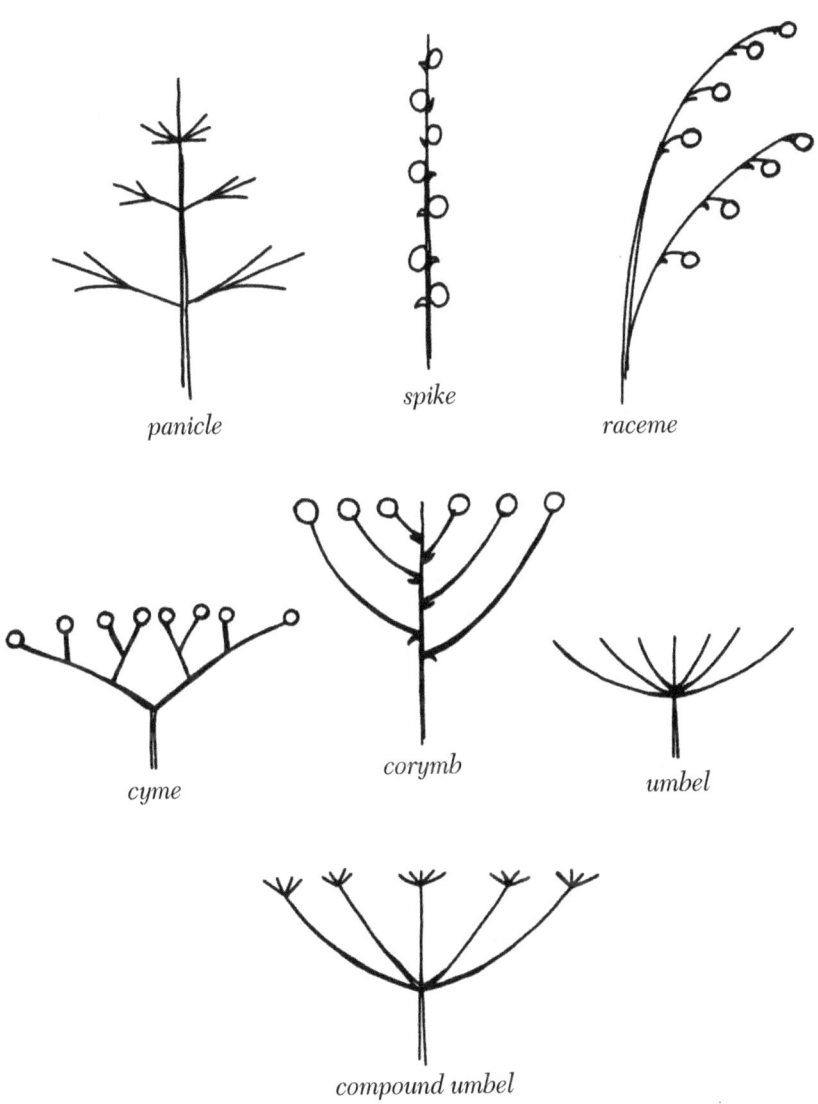

panicle

spike

raceme

cyme

corymb

umbel

compound umbel

GLOSSARY

achene. A one-seeded, dry fruit.
acuminate. Gradually tapering to a point.
acute. Sharply tapering to a point.
auricle. An ear-like lobe.
awn. A bristle usually terminating a structure.
bract. An accessory structure at the base of many flowers, usually appearing leaflike.
calyx. All the sepals of a flower.
catkin. A spike of unisexual flowers without petals.
ciliate. Bearing marginal hairs.
connate. Union of like parts.
cordate. Heart-shaped.
corolla. That part of the flower composed of the petals.
corona. A crown of petal-like structures.
corymb. A cluster of flowers where the stalked flowers are arranged along an elongated axis but with the flowers all attaining about the same height.
corymbose. Having a corymb.
culm. A stem which has one or more flowers at its end (usually refers to grasses and sedges).
cyme. A type of broad and flat cluster of flowers in which the central flowers bloom first.
dentate. With sharp teeth which project outward.
discoid. Having only disk flowers.
entire. Said of a leaf edge which has no teeth.
floret. A small flower.
glomerule. A small compact cluster.

glume. A sterile scale subtending a spikelet.
hastate. Spear-shaped.
head. A congested cluster of sessile flowers.
inferior. Referring to the position of the ovary when it is embedded in the receptacle.
inflorescence. A cluster of flowers.
involute. Rolled inward.
lanceolate. Lance-shaped.
lemma. A scale subtending a grass flower.
ligule. A structure on the inner surface of the leaf of a grass at the junction of the blade and sheath.
linear. Narrowly elongated and uniform in width throughout.
neutral. Said of a flower which has neither stamens nor pistils.
oblanceolate. Reversely lance-shaped.
oblong. Broadest at the middle and tapering to both ends, but broader than elliptic.
obovate. Reversely egg-shaped.
obtuse. Rounded.
orbicular. Round.
oval. Broadly elliptic.
ovary. The lower swollen part of the pistil.
ovate. Egg-shaped.
ovoid. A solid object which is egg-shaped.
palmate. Divided radiately like the fingers of a hand.
panicle. A cluster of flowers arranged in a series of racemes.
pedicel. The stalk of a flower.

GLOSSARY

peduncle. The stalk of a cluster of flowers.
perfect. Said of a flower which has both stamens and pistils.
perfoliate. Referring to a leaf which appears to have the stem pass through it.
perianth. Those parts of a flower including the sepals and petals.
petiolate. Having a leaf-stalk.
petiole. The stalk of a leaf.
pinnate. Divided once into distinct stamens.
pinnatifid. Said of a simple leaf which is cleft or lobed only part way to its axis.
pistillate. Referring to the pistil parts of the plant.
plumose. Feathery.
pubescence. Hairiness.
pubescent. Hairy.
raceme. A cluster of flowers whose stalked flowers are arranged along an elongated axis.
racemose. Having a raceme.
rachis. The axis to which the flowers are attached.
receptacle. That part of the flower to which the perianth, stamens, and pistils are usually attached.
reniform. Kidney-shaped.
rhizome. A horizontal, underground stem.
rosette. A cluster of leaves in a circular arrangement at the base of a plant.
scabrous. Rough to the touch.

scape. A leafless stalk bearing a flower or inflorescence.
serrate. With teeth which project forward.
serrulate. With small teeth which project forward.
sessile. Without a stalk.
spatulate. Oblong, but with the basal end elongated.
spicate. Possessing a spike.
spike. A cluster of flowers where sessile flowers are arranged along an elongated axis.
spikelet. A small spike.
stamen. The pollen-producing organ of the flower.
staminate. Referring to the pollen-producing parts of the plant.
stipule. A leaf-like structure found at the point of attachment of a leaf to the stem.
style. The elongated part of the pistil between the pistil and the stigma.
terete. Round in cross-section.
ternately. Divided into three parts.
tomentum. Wool.
trifoliolate. With 3 leaflets.
umbel. A flower cluster where all the flower stalks arise from the same level.
umbellate. Possessing an umbel.
verticillate. Whorled. viscid. Sticky.
whorl. An arrangement of three or more structures at a point on the stem.

KEY TO THE GROUPS OF PRAIRIE PLANTS

1. Plants with leaves long and narrow, at least ten times longer than broad; leaves with parallel veins 2
1. Plants with leaves usually not ten times longer than broad (if leaves are ten times longer than broad, then the leaves with net veins) . . . 3
   2. Plants with conspicuous flower parts, these either yellow, lavender, purple, white, or blue . . . . **GROUP E**, page 27
   2. Plants with inconspicuous green or straw-colored or brownish flowers having no petals . . . . **GROUP F**, page 29
3. All leaves confined to the base of the plant . . . . **GROUP A**, page 19
3. Leaves borne along the stem, although basal leaves may also be present 4
   4. Leaves, or some of them, compound, that is, divided into 3 or more distinct segments, or leaflets . . . . **GROUP B**, page 20
   4. Leaves all simple, that is, not divided into distinct segments, or leaflets, although the leaves may be lobed 5
5. Leaves whorled or opposite on the stem . . . . **GROUP C**, page 22
5. Leaves alternate on the stem . . . . **GROUP D**, page 24

NOTE: In the species descriptions following the keys, plants are arranged within each group alphabetically by their scientific name.

GROUP A

All the leaves confined to the base of the plant; leaves not long and narrow, never ten times longer than broad.

1. Some or all of the leaves compound, that is, divided into distinct segments, or leaflets 2
1. Leaves all simple, although sometimes toothed or lobed 3
    2. Leaflets 3, 1 cm or more wide; flowers white .... **WILD STRAWBERRY** (*Fragaria virginiana*, p. 37)
    2. Leaflets several, very narrow, always less than 5 mm wide; flowers purple .... **PRAIRIE VIOLET** (*Viola pedatifida*, p. 43)
3. Leaves deeply palmately divided into numerous narrow lobes .... **PRAIRIE VIOLET** (*Viola pedatifida*, p. 43)
3. Leaves not deeply lobed, although sometimes with a large tooth on either side near the base 4
    4. Leaves large, 15 or more cm wide, rough to the touch; flowers borne in yellow heads .... **PRAIRIE DOCK** .... (*Silphium terebinthinaceum*, p. 41)
    4. Leaves less than 10 cm across, not rough to the touch, although sometimes hairy; flowers not borne in yellow heads 5
5. Leaves without any teeth, tapering gradually into broad petioles; petals pointing backward...................... **SHOOTING-STAR** .... (*Dodecatheon meadia*, p. 35)
5. Leaves toothed or with broad scallops around the margin, or with a large tooth on either side near the base 6
    6. Leaves with broad scallops around the margin; flowers very small, greenish .... **ROUGH HEUCHERA** .... (*Heuchera richardsonii*, p. 39)
    6. Leaves with toothed margins; flowers up to 2 cm across, purple 7
7. Leaves with a large tooth on either side near the base .... **ARROW-LEAVED VIOLET** (*Viola sagittata*, p. 45)
7. Leaves without a large tooth at base .... **BLUE VIOLET** .... (*Viola sororia*, p. 47)

GROUP B

Leaves, or some of them, compound, that is, divided into 3 or more distinct segments or leaflets.

1. Flowers white or cream-colored 2
1. Flowers yellow, blue, lavender, rose, purple, or pink 8
   2. Leaves divided into divided into 3, 5, or 7 segments 3
   2. Leaves divided into 9 or more segments, or leaflets ....
      .... **WATER HEMLOCK** (*Cicuta maculata*, p. 63)
3. Flowers shaped like little sweet peas, asymmetrical; leaflets without teeth along the edges 4
3. Flowers with 5-several petal-like sepals surrounding a central core of pistils, symmetrical; leaflets usually with some irregular teeth .. 7
   4. Leaflets 5-7; flowers small, in densely crowded spikes ....
      .... **WHITE PRAIRIE CLOVER** (*Dalea candida*, p. 65)
   4. Leaflets 3; flowers at least 7 mm long, less crowded in an elongated inflorescence 5
5. Flowers up to 1 cm long, with a purple dot ..... **BUSH LESPEDEZA**
   .... (*Lespedeza capitata*, p. 71)
5. Flowers over 1 cm long, without a purple dot 6
   6. Plants smooth; pods smooth, up to 3 cm long ....
      .... **WHITE FALSE INDIGO** (*Baptisia alba*, p. 57)
   6. Plants usually hairy; pods hairy, usually at least 4 cm long ....
      .... **WILD FALSE INDIGO** (*Baptisia bracteata*, p. 59)
7. Plants arising from a tuber; petal-like sepals 10-20 ....
   .... **CAROLINA ANEMONE** (*Anemone caroliniana*, p. 55)
7. Plants arising from a rhizome; petal-like sepals 5 (-6) ....
   .... **CANADIAN ANEMONE** (*Anemone canadensis*, p. 53)
   8. Flowers yellow 9
   8. Flowers blue, lavender, purple, rose, or pink 12
9. Flowers borne in heads, with several yellow rays surrounding an elongated central column .... **DROOPING CONEFLOWER**
   .... (*Ratibida pinnata*, p. 83)
9. Flowers borne in loose clusters, in umbels, or solitary 10
   10. Flowers solitary or in small clusters; each flower more than 1 cm across; stamens 10 .... **PARTRIDGE PEA**
       .... (*Chamaecrista fasciculata*, p. 61)
   10. Flowers borne in umbels; each flower less than 1 cm across; stamens 5 11

GROUP B, *continued*

Leaves, or some of them, compound, that is, divided into 3 or more distinct segments or leaflets.

11. Leaflets uniform-shaped . . **GOLDEN ALEXANDERS** (*Zizia aurea*, p. 91)
11. Leaflets highly dissected, not uniformly shaped. . . **PRAIRIE PARSLEY** . . . . (*Polytaenia nuttallii*, p. 79)
    12. Plants woody with some prickles on the stem; flowers rose-colored . . . . **CAROLINA ROSE** (*Rosa carolina*, p. 85)
    12. Plants herbaceous (woody near base in *Amorpha canescens*), without prickles on the stem; flowers blue, lavender, purple, or pink and cream 13
13. Leaflets 3 or 5 14
13. Leaflets 7 to many 17
    14. Leaflets with a few glandular dots (best seen by holding leaf to light) 15
    14. Leaflets without glandular dots 16
15. Leaflets always 3 . . . . **SAMPSON'S SNAKEROOT** . . . . (*Orbexilum psoralioides*, p. 75)
15. Leaflets sometimes 5 . . . **SCURF PEA** (*Pediomelum tenuiflorum*, p. 77)
    16. Flowers in an elongated, cylindrical head; leaflets sometimes 5 . . . . **WHITE PRAIRIE CLOVER** (*Dalea purpurea*, p. 67)
    16. Flowers loosely clustered; leaflets always 3. . . . . **VIRGINIA LESPEDEZA** (*Lespedeza virginica*, p. 73)
17. Flowers pea-shaped 18
17. Flowers not pea-shaped, symmetrical 20
    18. Flowers pink and cream; leaves with an uneven number of leaflets . . . . **GOAT'S-RUE** (*Tephrosia virginiana*, p. 87)
    18. Flowers bluish-purple; leaves with an uneven or even number of leaflets 19
19. Plants shrub-like, grayish, leaflets uneven in number . . . . **LEADPLANT** (*Amorpha canescens*, p. 51)
19. Plants trailing and herbaceous, green; leaflets even in number, the leaf usually tipped by tendrils. . . . . **AMERICAN VETCH** . . . . (*Vicia americana*, p. 89)
    20. Leaves palmately divided . . . . **PASQUE-FLOWER** . . . . (*Pulsatilla patens*, p. 81)
    20. Leaves pinnately divided, with small leaf segments between the regular leaflets . . . . **PRAIRIE-SMOKE** (*Geum triflorum*, p. 69)

GROUP C

Leaves simple, opposite or whorled.

1. Leaves whorled 2
1. Leaves opposite 4
    2. Leaves toothed; flowers in an elongated, candelabra-like inflorescence CULVER'S-ROOT (*Veronicastrum virginicum*, p. 141)
    2. Leaves entire; flowers in umbels or racemes 3
3. Flowers in umbels; latex present .... WHORLED MILKWEED .... (*Asclepias verticillata*, p. 99)
3. Flowers in racemes; latex absent .... STIFF MARSH BEDSTRAW .... (*Galium tinctorium*, p. 107)
    4. Flowers with an hour-glass shape; latex present 5
    4. Flowers not with an hour-glass shape; latex absent 7
5. Flowers purple; leaves broadly rounded or subcordate at the base . ... SULLIVANT'S MILKWEED (*Asclepias sullivantii*, p. 97)
5. Flowers greenish; leaves tapering to the base 6
    6. Each umbel of flowers borne on an elongated stalk .... HAIRY GREEN MILKWEED (*Asclepias hirtella*, p. 95)
    6. Each umbel of flowers sessile or nearly so . . GREEN MILKWEED .... (*Asclepias viridiflora*, p. 101)
7. Flowers yellow 8
7. Flowers deep blue, pink, purple, or white with purple dots 16
    8. Flowers borne single, with distinct yellow petals .... FRINGED LOOSESTRIFE (*Lysimachia ciliata*, p. 123)
    8. Flowers borne several in a head, the head usually composed of several tubular flowers in a central disk, surrounded by several ray flowers 9
9. Leaves deeply 3-lobed . STIFF TICKSEED (*Coreopsis palmata*, p. 105)
9. Leaves without lobes 10
    10. Each flower head with several rows of green leaf-like bracts on the outside 11
    10. Each flower head with 1 or 2 rows of green leaf-like bracts on the outside 12
11. Leaves completely clasping the stem so as to form cup-shaped cavities .... CUP-PLANT (*Silphium perfoliatum*, p. 137)

GROUP C, *continued*

Leaves simple, opposite or whorled.

11. Leaves sessile or short petiolate, but never clasping the stem . . . . **ROSINWEED** (*Silphium integrifolium*, p. 135)
    12. Leaf-like bracts on the outside of each flower head obtuse; ray flowers fertile, long persistent . . . . **FALSE SUNFLOWER** . . . . (*Heliopsis helianthoides*, p. 121)
    12. Leaf-like bracts on the outside of each flower head acute; ray flowers sterile, not long persistent 13
13. Central disk of each flower head red or purple . . **STIFF SUNFLOWER** . . . . (*Helianthus pauciflorus*, p. 113)
13. Central disk of each flower head yellow 14
    14. Stems smooth or nearly so below the flower heads . . . . **SAWTOOTH SUNFLOWER** (*Helianthus grosseserratus*, p. 115)
    14. Stems hairy 15
15. Leaves densely gray-hairy on both surfaces . . . . **HAIRY SUNFLOWER** . . . . (*Helianthus mollis*, p. 117)
15. Leaves not densely gray-hairy, although they may have some hairs . . . . **JERUSALEM ARTICHOKE** (*Helianthus tuberosus*, p. 119)
    16. Flowers white, with purple dots 17
    16. Flowers pink, blue, or purple 18
17. Stems smooth; leaves up to 5 mm broad . . . . **MOUNTAIN MINT** . . . . (*Pycnanthemum tenuifolium*, p. 129)
17. Stems hairy; leaves (or most of them) over 5 mm broad . . . . **PRAIRIE HYSSOP** (*Pycnanthemum virginianum*, p. 131)
    18. Flowers 2-lipped, distinctly asymmetrical 19
    18. Flowers not 2-lipped, mostly symmetrical 20
19. Flowers crowded in dense globular heads nearly as wide as high, or wider . . . . **WILD BERGAMOT** (*Monarda fistulosa*, p. 125)
19. Flowers clustered in an elongated spike considerably longer than broad . . . . **AMERICAN GERMANDER** (*Teucrium canadense*, p. 139)
    20. Leaves toothed; flowers slightly asymmetrical . . . . **BLUE HEARTS** (*Buchnera americana*, p. 103)
    20. Leaves entire; flowers perfectly symmetrical 21
21. Stamens 4 . . . . **WILD PETUNIA** (*Ruellia humilis*, p. 133)
21. Stamens 5 22

GROUP C, *continued*

Leaves simple, opposite or whorled.

22. Corolla abruptly narrowed below the lobes into a very slender tube . . . . **PRAIRIE PHLOX** (*Phlox pilosa*, p. 127)
22. Corolla scarcely tapering below the lobes 23
23. Stems hairy; corolla open at the top . . . . **DOWNY GENTIAN** . . . . (*Gentiana puberulenta*, p. 111)
23. Stems smooth; corolla nearly closed at the top . . . . **CLOSED GENTIAN** (*Gentiana andrewsii*, p. 109)

GROUP D

Leaves simple, alternate.

1. Flowers crowded together in a head, each flower sharing a common receptacle 2
1. Flowers borne individually, each with its own receptacle 24
    2. Flowers white, whitish-green, or cream 3
    2. Flowers blue, purple, violet, or yellow 8
3. Heads composed of both ray flowers and disk flowers 4
3. Heads composed only of disk flowers 5
    4. Rays 15-25, usually at least 1 cm long; leaves linear to linear-lanceolate . . . **HEATH ASTER** (*Symphyotrichum ericoides*, p. 201)
    4. Rays 5, less than 1 cm long; leaves ovate to ovate-oblong . . . . **AMERICAN FEVERFEW** (*Parthenium intergrifolium*, p. 189)
5. Leaves (at least the lower surface) and stems covered with dense white wool 6
5. Leaves and stems not white-woolly 7
    6. Most of the leaves clustered in a basal rosette; leaves on the stem linear; heads 4-6 mm across . . . . **PUSSY-TOES** . . . . (*Antennaria neglecta*, p. 145)
    6. Leaves not clustered in a basal rosette; leaves on the stem lanceolate to oblong; heads 2-3 mm across . . . . . . **PRAIRIE SAGE** . . . . (*Artemisia ludoviciana*, p. 147)

GROUP D, *continued*

Leaves simple, alternate.

7. Plants smooth; lower leaves oval to ovate, long petiolate; upper leaves ovate to oblong, sessile ....
.... INDIAN PLANTAIN (*Arnoglossum plantagineum*, p. 149)
7. Plants hairy; all leaves similar, lanceolate to linear-lanceolate .....
.... FALSE BONESET (*Brickellia eupatorioides*, p. 157)
    8. Flowers purple or pink 9
    8. Flowers yellow 17
9. Heads with both ray and disk flowers....................... 10
9. Heads with only disk flowers............................... 15
    10. Rays pink, turned downward; disk conical, brownish-black ...
.... PALE PRAIRIE CONEFLOWER (*Echinacea pallida*, p. 165)
    10. Rays purple, spreading; disk flat, yellow 11
11. Basal or lowest leaves heart-shaped .... SKY-BLUE ASTER
.... (*Symphyotrichum oolentangiense*, p. 209)
11. Basal or lowest leaves not heart-shaped 12
    12. Stem-leaves not clasping at the base .... SILKY ASTER
.... (*Symphyotrichum sericeum*, p. 211)
    12. Stem-leaves clasping at the base 13
13. Stems smooth ..... SMOOTH ASTER (*Symphyotrichum laeve*, p. 203)
13. Stems hairy, at least in the upper part 14
    14. Leaves strongly clasping; rays 40 or more NEW ENGLAND ASTER
.... (*Symphyotrichum novae-angliae*, p. 205)
    14. Leaves barely clasping; rays usually 20-30 ... AROMATIC ASTER
.... (*Symphyotrichum oblongifolium*, p. 207)
15. Heads in a dense spike 15 cm or more long .... TALL GAYFEATHER
.... (*Liatris pycnostachya*, p. 177)
15. Heads usually solitary in the axils of the leaves, 1-3 cm long 16
    16. Bracts on outside of flower heads rounded at the tip, appressed
.... ROUGH BLAZING-STAR (*Liatris aspera*, p. 175)
    16. Bracts on outside of flower heads pointed at the tip, projecting outward .... SCALY BLAZING-STAR (*Liatris squarrosa*, p. 179)
17. All leaves deeply pinnately lobed, the leaves usually 15 cm or more broad .... COMPASS PLANT (*Silphium laciniatum*, p. 195)
17. Leaves unlobed or only shallowly lobed, never 15 cm broad 18

GROUP D, *continued*

Leaves simple, alternate.

18. Basal leaves unlobed, stem-leaves shallowly lobed ....
    .... **PRAIRIE GROUNDSEL** (*Packera paupercula*, p. 187)
18. All leaves unlobed 19
19. Heads with yellow rays 1 cm or more long 20
19. Heads with yellow rays rarely longer than 5 mm 22
    20. Heads with a brown-black, low-conical center ....
        .... **BROWN-EYED SUSAN** (*Rudbeckia hirta*, p. 191)
    20. Heads with a yellow, flattened center 21
21. Stems smooth or nearly so .... **SAWTOOTH SUNFLOWER**
    .... (*Helianthus grosseserratus*, p. 171)
21. Stems hairy .. **JERUSALEM ARTICHOKE** (*Helianthus tuberosus*, p. 173)
    22. Leaves linear to linear-lanceolate, up to 6 mm wide ....
        . **GRASS-LLEAVED GOLDENROD** (*Euthamnia graminifolia*, p. 169)
    22. Leaves ovate, elliptic, lanceolate, or oblanceolate 23
23. Leaves lanceolate or oblanceolate, strongly 3-nerved from the base
    .... **TALL GOLDENROD** (*Solidago canadensis*, p. 197)
23. Leaves ovate to elliptic, not conspicuously 3-nerved from the base
    .... **STIFF GOLDENROD** (*Solidago rigida*, p. 199)
    24. Plants with latex (white sap) 25
    24. Plants without latex 27
25. Flowers white, not hour-glass shaped ...... **FLAT-TOPPED SPURGE**
    .... (*Euphorbia corollata*, p. 167)
25. Flowers green, hour-glass shaped 26
    26. Each umbel of flowers borne on an elongated stalk ....
        .... **HAIRY GREEN MILKWEED** (*Asclepias hirtella*, p. 151)
    26. Each umbel of flowers sessile or nearly so ....
        .... **GREEN MILKWEED** (*Asclepias viridiflora*, p. 155)
27. Plants small shrubs 28
27. Plants herbaceous; flowers with petals or petal-like structures .. 29
    28. Leaves with one main vein .... **PRAIRIE WILLOW**
        .... (*Salix humilis*, p. 193)
    28. Leaves with three veins from the base, all about the same size .
        .... **NEW JERSEY TEA** (*Ceanothus americana*, p. 161)
29. Flowers orange or yellow 30

GROUP D, *continued*

Leaves simple, alternate.

29. Flowers purple, pale blue, or cream 32
    30. Flowers hour-glass shaped, orange .... **BUTTERFLY WEED** .... (*Asclepias tuberosa*, p. 153)
    30. Flowers not hour-glass shaped, yellow to yellow-orange 31
31. Petals 4, free from each other, yellow; flowers 2 cm or more across .... **COMMON SUNDROPS** (*Oenothera pilosella*, p. 185)
31. Petals 5, attached to each other, yellow-orange; flowers less than 2 cm across ...... **HOARY PUCCOON** (*Lithospermum canescens*, p. 181)
    32. Flowers purple; leaves triangular, large .... **CLUSTERED POPPY MALLOW** (*Callirhoe triangulata*, p. 159)
    32. Flowers cream-colored or light blue; leaves not triangular, small 33
33. Flowers cream-colored, borne in umbel-like inflorescences .... **FALSE TOADFLAX** (*Comandra umbellata*, p. 163)
33. Flowers pale blue, borne in a spike .... **SPIKED LOBELIA** .... (*Lobelia spicata*, p. 183)

GROUP E

Leaves long and narrow, at least ten times longer than broad; leaves with parallel veins; flowers showy, yellow, lavender, purple, blue, orange, or white.

1. Leaves with spine-like teeth; flowers white, borne in spherical heads .... **RATTLESNAKE MASTER** (*Eryngium yuccifolium*, p. 217)
1. Leaves without teeth; flowers variously colored but not white, not borne in spherical heads 2
    2. Flowers yellow or orange 3
    2. Flowers blue, purple, or lavender 5
3. Flowers yellow, up to 2 cm across; leaves all basal, hairy .... **YELLOW STAR-GRASS** (*Hypoxis hirsuta*, p. 219)
3. Flowers orange, more than 4 cm across; leaves borne on the stem 4

GROUP E, *continued*

Leaves long and narrow, at least ten times longer than broad; leaves with parallel veins; flowers showy, yellow, lavender, purple, blue, orange, or white.

    4. Flowers erect; only the uppermost group of leaves in a whorl; plants less than 1 meter tall .... **WESTERN LILY** .... (***Lilium philadelphicum***, p. 227)

    4. Flowers nodding; several whorls of leaves borne on the stem; plants generally over 1 meter tall .... **TURK'S-CAP LILY** .... (***Lilium michiganense***, p. 225)

5. Flowers large, 5 cm or more across, with petal-like styles 6
5. Flowers small, up to 2.5 cm across, with the styles not petal-like .. 7

    6. Flowers borne on erect stems; ovary and fruit 3-angled .... **VIRGINIA BLUE FLAG** (***Iris virginica***, p. 223)

    6. Flowers borne near the ground; ovary and fruit 6-angled .... **ZIGZAG IRIS** (***Iris brevicaulis***, p. 221)

7. Stems winged; stamens 3; ovary inferior .... **NARROW-LEAVED BLUE-EYED GRASS** .... (***Sisyrinchium angustifolium***, p. 229)
7. Stems unwinged; stamens 6; ovary superior 8

    8. Sepals and petals the same color; stalks bearing the anthers smooth .... **WILD HYACINTH** (***Camassia scilloides***, p. 215)

    8. Sepals green, petals blue or lavender; stalks bearing the anthers with long hairs 9

9. Stems generally 40-100 cm tall; leaves and stems glabrous and glaucous; sepals glabrous or with a tuft of eglandular hairs at the tip .... **SPIDERWORT** (***Tradescantia ohiensis***, p. 233)

9. Stems generally 5-40 cm tall; leaves and stems glabrous or pubescent, but not glaucous; sepals pubescent throughout with glandular or eglandular hairs 10

    10. Hairs of the sepals eglandular .... **COMMON SPIDERWORT** .... (***Tradescantia virginiana***, p. 235)

    10. Hairs of the sepals glandular .... **PRAIRIE SPIDERWORT** .... (***Tradescantia bracteata***, p. 231)

GROUP F

Leaves long and narrow, at least ten times longer than broad; leaves with parallel veins; flowers inconspicuous, green or brown or straw-colored, without petals.

1. Leaves borne in 3 ranks; staminate flowers borne separately from pistillate flowers 2
1. Leaves borne in 2 ranks; staminate flowers and pistillate flowers borne together (except in *Tripsacum dactyloides*) 3
    2. Fruiting structures hairy .... **PENNSYLVANIA SEDGE** .... (*Carex pensylvanica*, p. 243)
    2. Fruiting structures smooth .... **MEAD'S SEDGE** .... (*Carex meadii*, p. 245)
3. Spikelets bearing six perianth parts 4
3. Spikelets without perianth parts; the flowers, instead, subtended by scales 5
    4. Flowers borne in spherical heads; plants over 50 cm tall .... **TORREY'S RUSH** (*Juncus torreyi*, p. 257)
    4. Flowers borne along an elongated axis; plants usually less than 30 cm tall .... **PATH RUSH** (*Juncus tenuis*, p. 255)
5. Staminate and pistillate flowers borne separately; leaves 15-30 mm broad .... **EASTERN GAMA GRASS** (*Tripsacum dactyloides*, p. 279)
5. Staminate and pistillate flowers borne together; leaves rarely over 15 mm broad 6
    6. Spikelets bearing one or more awns (bristle- or thread-like extensions from the apex) at least 3 mm long 7
    6. Spikelets without awns 14
7. Spikelets arranged in unbranched, dense spikes 8
7. Spikelets arranged in racemes or panicles (these sometimes condensed) 9
    8. Spikes 10-25 cm long; awns usually more than 15 mm long; plants perennial, to 2 meters tall .... **NODDING WILD RYE** .... (*Elymus canadensis*, p. 249)
    8. Spikes 2-7 cm long; awns less than 15 mm long; plants annual, to 35 cm tall .... **LITTLE WILD BARLEY** (*Hordeum pusillum*, p. 253)
9. Plants annual, up to 50 cm tall; leaves about 1 mm broad .... **SIX-WEEKS FESCUE** (*Vulpia octoflora*, p. 281)

GROUP F, *continued*

Leaves long and narrow, at least ten times longer than broad; leaves with parallel veins; flowers inconspicuous, green or brown or straw-colored, without petals.

9. Plants perennial, more than 50 cm tall; leaves 3-15 mm broad .. 10
    - 10. Spikelets borne in pairs, although one member of each pair may be reduced merely to a stalk 11
    - 10. Spikelets borne singly, that is, not in pairs 13
11. One spikelet of a pair represented only by a bristly stalk .... **INDIAN GRASS** (*Sorghastrum nutans*, p. 269)
11. Both spikelets of a pair present 12
    - 12. Each branch of the inflorescence terminated by a single raceme .... **LITTLE BLUESTEM** (*Schizachyrium scoparium*)
    - 12. Each branch in the inflorescence terminated by 2-4 racemes .. .. **BIG BLUESTEM** (*Andropogon gerardii*, p. 239)
13. Spikelets borne in 1-sided racemes, the spikelets 10-25 mm long; leaves usually 8-15 mm wide .... **PRAIRIE CORDGRASS** .... (*Sporobolus michauxianus*, p. 277)
13. Spikelets borne in open panicles, the spikelets 28-42 mm long; leaves usually 4-6 mm wide .. **NEEDLEGRASS** (*Hesperostipa spartea*, p. 251)
    - 14. Spikelets 2- or more-flowered 15
    - 14. Spikelets 1-flowered 18
15. Plants annual, usually up to 35 cm tall (rarely to 50 cm) .... **SIX-WEEKS FESCUE** (*Vulpia octoflora*, p. 281)
15. Plants perennial, regularly more than 35 cm tall 16
    - 16. . Spikelets 7-10 mm long, borne on one side of the inflorescence .... **SIDE-OATS GRAMA** (*Bouteloua curtipendula*, p. 241)
    - 16. Spikelets 3-6 mm long, borne on various sides of the inflorescence 17
17. Inflorescence appearing to be spike-like .... **JUNE GRASS** .... (*Koeleria macrantha*, p. 259)
17. Inflorescence an open panicle .... **KENTUCKY BLUEGRASS** .... (*Poa pratensis*, p. 265)
    - 18. Panicle contracted and nearly spike-like, mostly concealed by a sheath .... **TALL DROPSEED** (*Sporobolus compositus*, p. 271)
    - 18. Panicle open, not concealed by a sheath 19

GROUP F, *continued*

Leaves long and narrow, at least ten times longer than broad; leaves with parallel veins; flowers inconspicuous, green or brown or straw-colored, without petals.

19. Leaves 1 mm wide or less, rolled up along edges ....
.... PRAIRIE DROPSEED (*Sporobolus heterolepis*, p. 275)
19. Leaves 2-15 mm wide, flat 21

    20. Spikelets blunt and rounded at the tip, hairy ....
    .. SCRIBNER'S PANIC GRASS (*Dichanthelium oligosanthes*, p. 247)
    20. Spikelets pointed at the tip, smooth 21

21. Leaves 2-6 mm wide; all scales of the spikelets similar in shape and texture .... SAND DROPSEED (*Sporobolus cryptandrus*, p. 273)
21. Leaves usually 8-15 mm wide; one of the scales of the spikelet much smaller than the others 22

    22. Spikelets 2.0-2.5 mm long; plants mostly 1-2 meters tall ......
    .... SWITCHGRASS (*Panicum virgatum*, p. 263)
    22. Spikelets 3.5-6.0 mm long; plants up to 75 cm tall ....
    .... WITCH GRASS (*Panicum capillare*, p. 261)

Prairie dominated by big bluestem (*Andropogon gerardii*); tall gayfeather (*Liatris pycnostachya*) and drooping coneflower (*Ratibida pinnata*) are also present.

GROUP A

SHOOTING-STAR (*Dodecatheon meadia*), see p. 35

GROUP A

All the leaves confined to the base of the plant; leaves not long and narrow, never ten times longer than broad.

SHOOTING-STAR (*Dodecatheon meadia*), p. 35
WILD STRAWBERRY (*Fragaria virginiana*), p. 37
ROUGH HEUCHERA (*Heuchera richardsonii*), p. 39
PRAIRIE DOCK (*Silphium terebinthinaceum*), p. 41
PRAIRIE VIOLET (*Viola pedatifida*), p. 43
ARROW-LEAVED VIOLET (*Viola sagittata*), p. 45
BLUE VIOLET (*Viola sororia*), p. 47

SHOOTING-STAR
Dodecatheon meadia L.

SHOOTING-STAR
Dodecatheon meadia L.

Synonym *Primula meadia* (L.) A.R. Mast & Reveal

Family Primulaceae, or Primrose Family

Season and Stature Shooting-star is a native, cool-season perennial. It grows to 60 cm and blooms during Spring.

Flowers The flowers, which are few to several in umbels, are purplish to usually pink or whitish. The calyx is deeply 5-lobed; petals are 5, with reflexed lobes.

Leaves Basal, oblanceolate, narrowed into margined petioles, pale green, 7 to 20 cm long, and 1.5 to 6 cm wide.

Use or Importance Shooting-star is an attractive plant which has been grown successfully in gardens.

Habitat Prairies, moist slopes, rocky hillsides.

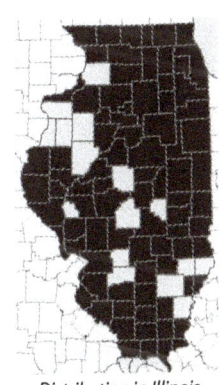
Distribution in Illinois

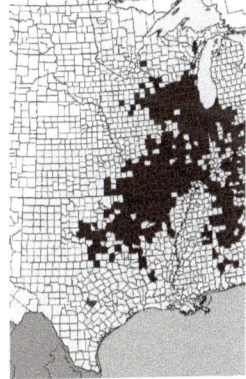
Distribution in central USA

Group A. All leaves confined to the base of the plant; leaves not long and narrow, never ten times longer than broad.

WILD STRAWBERRY

A

Fragaria virginiana P. Mill.

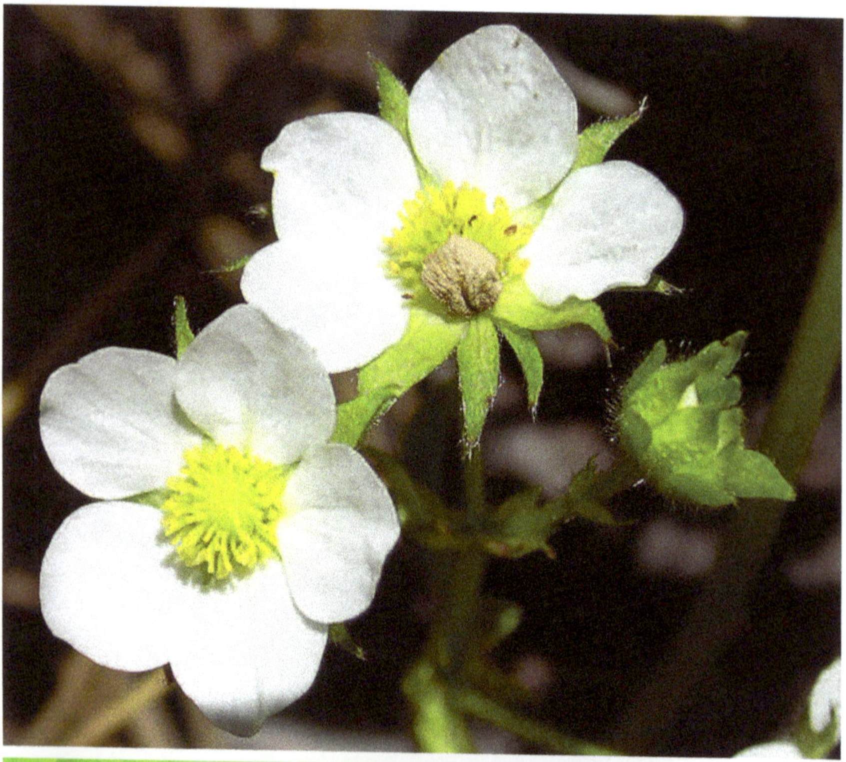

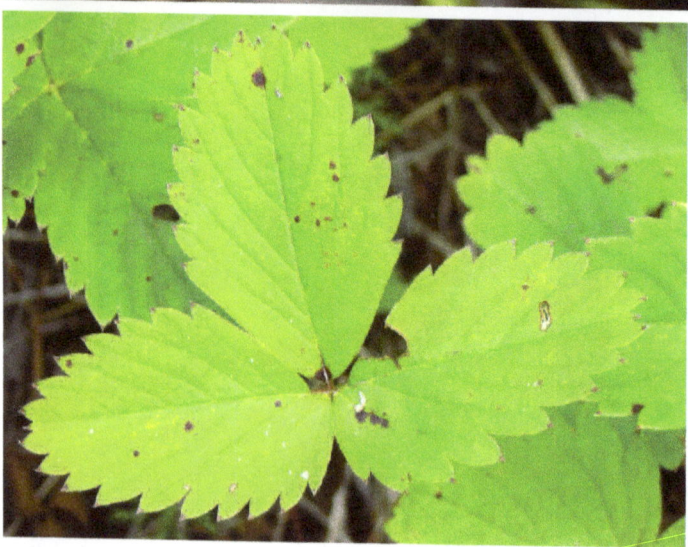

WILD STRAWBERRY

Fragaria virginiana P. Mill.

From L. *fraga*, strawberry; deriving from *fragrans*, fragrant, in allusion to the perfume of the fruit.

Family Rosaceae, or Rose Family

Season and Stature Wild Strawberry is a native, cool-season perennial. It is a low-growing herb, flowering at about the level of its own leaves which grow to about 15 cm high.

Flowers The flowering stalks are about equal to or slightly shorter than the leaves. The petals are five and white; stamens numerous.

Leaves Dark green, 3-parted, on petioles to 15 cm long. The three leaflets are short stalked or sessile, oval to obovate, serrate.

Use or Importance Wild Strawberries are edible, but small.

Habitat Prairies, fields, woodland borders.

Distribution in Illinois

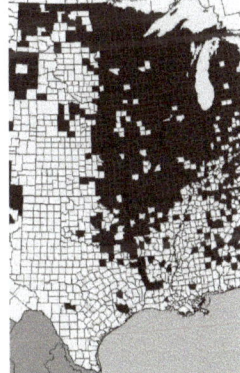

Distribution in central USA

Group A. All leaves confined to the base of the plant; leaves not long and narrow, never ten times longer than broad.

ROUGH HEUCHERA or ALUMROOT
Heuchera richardsonii R. Br.

ROUGH HEUCHERA or ALUMROOT

Heuchera richardsonii R. Br. In honor of Johann Heinrich von Heucher (1677-1747), Professor of Medicine at Wittenberg University.

Family Saxifragaceae, or Saxifrage Family

Season and Stature A native cool-season perennial species. It attains a height of over 60 cm and flowers during late Spring.

Flowers The inflorescence is narrowly paniculate. The calyx is cup-shaped and asymmetrical, 3 to 5 mm long. The petals are spatulate and longer than the calyx; the stamens extend beyond the petals. The flower color is greenish-cream.

Leaves Basal, ovate-orbicular, with have 5 to 9 shallow, rounded, coarsely toothed lobes. The stems are hairy.

Use or Importance Unknown importance apart from the native plant garden; never abundant where found.

Habitat Prairies, roadsides, and roadside prairie remnants. In Illinois, found in a variety of prairie types.

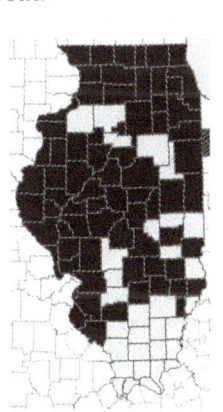 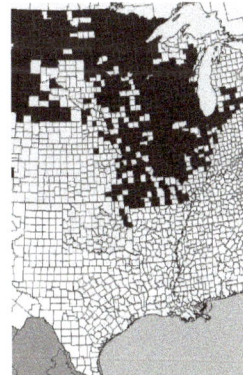

Distribution in Illinois   Distribution in central USA

Group A. All leaves confined to the base of the plant; leaves not long and narrow, never ten times longer than broad.

PRAIRIE DOCK

A

Silphium terebinthinaceum Jacq.

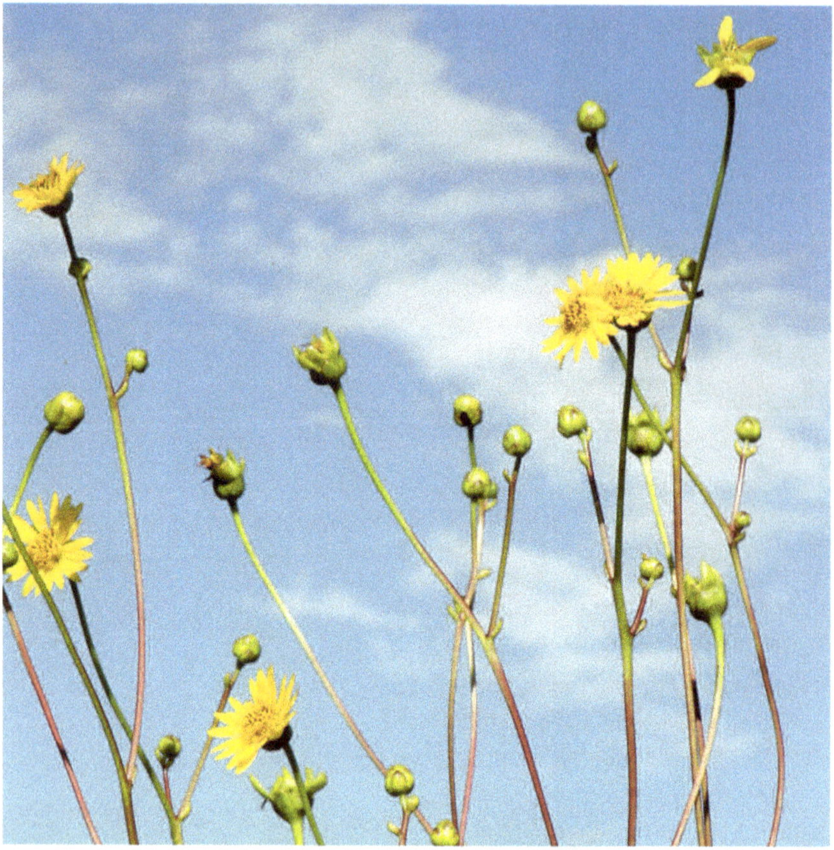

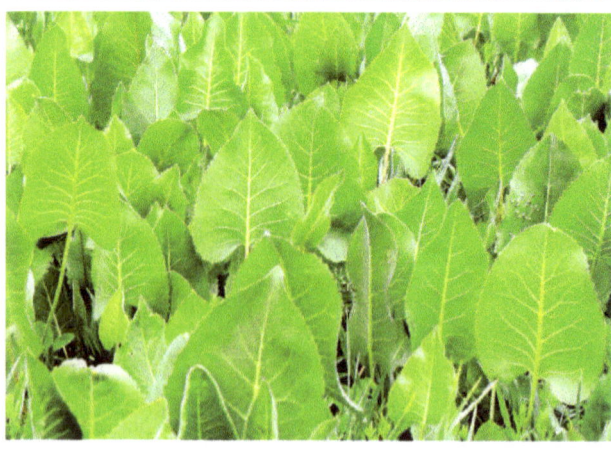

PRAIRIE DOCK

Silphium terebinthinaceum Jacq. Perennial herbs with the Greek name for another plant also producing resin.

Family Asteraceae, or Aster Family

Season and Stature Prairie Dock is a native, warm-season perennial herb. It is one of the four Illinois species of *Silphium*. The flowering stem often attains a height greater than 2 meters. Prairie Dock blooms during the late Summer-Fall.

Flowers The numerous, yellow heads have both ray and disk flowers. They range from 3.5 to 8 cm wide. The rays number from 12 to 20 per head.

Leaves Distinctive in that they are rough like sandpaper and are confined to the base of the plant. The leaves are broadly ovate, and cordate at the base. The blades are often more than 40 cm long and up to 30 cm wide.

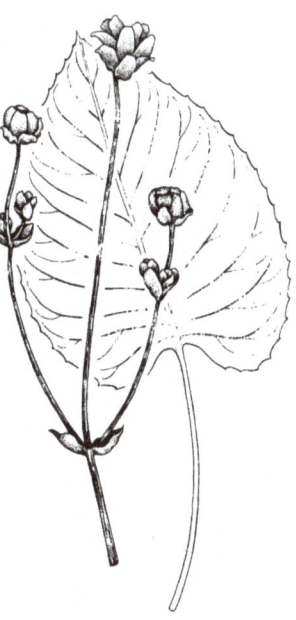

Use or Importance This species forms a gum or rosin which is used in various ways. It was chewed by early settlers as a gum. The plant is palatable in young growth and tends to decrease when the prairie is grazed.

Habitat A characteristic prairie species; forming roadside colonies.

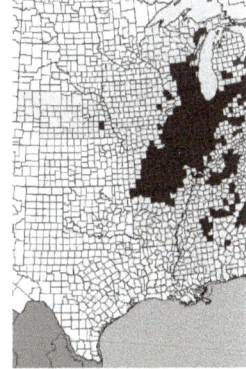

Distribution in Illinois Distribution in central USA

Group A. All leaves confined to the base of the plant; leaves not long and narrow, never ten times longer than broad.

PRAIRIE VIOLET
Viola pedatifida G. Don

PRAIRIE VIOLET

Viola pedatifida G. Don   The Latin name for these herbaceous annuals and perennials.

Family Violaceae, or Violet Family

Season and Stature Prairie Violet is a very early Spring bloomer, usually flowering before all but the cool-season grasses begin growth.

Flowers The violet-colored flowers are borne on erect peduncles which are shorter than the petioles of the leaves. The flowering stalks reach a height of 10 cm.

Leaves The leaves are palmately cleft, usually 3-parted, with each part again 3-cleft into linear divisions, with these again cut into 2 to 4 lobes.

Use or Importance Violets are usually noted only for their beauty; unique in being one of the earliest flowering prairie flowers.

Habitat Upland prairies.

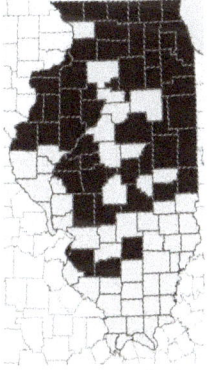
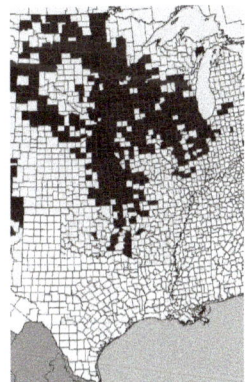

Distribution in Illinois   *Distribution in central USA*

Group A. All leaves confined to the base of the plant; leaves not long and narrow, never ten times longer than broad.

ARROW-LEAVED VIOLET
Viola sagittata Ait().

ARROW-LEAVED VIOLET

Viola sagittata Ait.

The Latin name for these herbaceous annuals and perennials.

Family Violaceae, or Violet Family

Season and Stature Arrow-leaved Violet is a native, cool-season species, which blooms during Spring.

Flowers The flowers are on peduncles about as long as the leaves. Each flower is violet-purple and up to 2.5 cm long.

Leaves The petioles of the leaves are usually longer than the blades, which are hastate, or spear-shaped and toothed or cleft below the middle.

Use or Importance Arrow-leaved Violet, like most other violets, is valued as an attractive, delicate, early blooming plant.

Habitat Characteristic of sandy prairies (although not restricted to that habitat); also found in moist places.

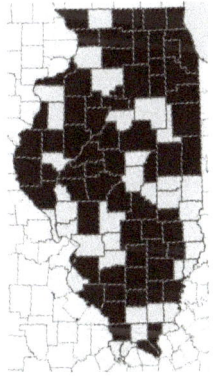

Distribution in Illinois

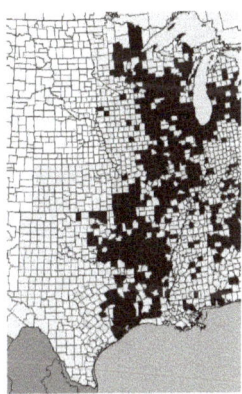

Distribution in central USA

Group A. All leaves confined to the base of the plant; leaves not long and narrow, never ten times longer than broad.

BLUE VIOLET
Viola sororia Willd.

BLUE VIOLET

Viola sororia Willd. The Latin name for these herbaceous annuals and perennials.

Family Violaceae, or Violet Family

Season and Stature This common Blue Violet is an early or cool-season native plant. It blooms during Spring. It attains a height of about 10 cm (or more).

Flowers Deep blue with a whitish center.

Leaves Reniform, ovate, cordate or abruptly pointed; smooth or hairy.

Use or Importance Violets are reported to have both edible flowers and leaves. The leaves are reported to be rich in vitamins A and C. Both leaves and flowers are mixed with other pot herbs. Tea from the leaves is, according to folk reports, purported to strengthen the heart and induce sleep. Blue Violet is the state flower of Illinois.

Habitat Woodlands, prairies, lawns.

  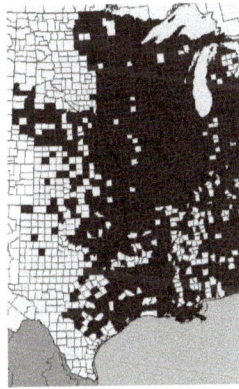

Distribution in Illinois   *Distribution in central USA*

Group A. All leaves confined to the base of the plant; leaves not long and narrow, never ten times longer than broad.

GROUP B

WHITE FALSE INDIGO (*Baptisia alba*), see p. 57

GROUP B

Leaves, or some of them, compound, that is, divided into 3 or more distinct segments or leaflets.

LEADPLANT (*Amorpha canescens*), p. 51
CANADIAN ANEMONE (*Anemone canadensis*), p. 53
CAROLINA ANEMONE (*Anemone caroliniana*), p. 55
WHITE FALSE INDIGO (*Baptisia alba*), p. 57
WILD FALSE INDIGO (*Baptisia bracteata*), p. 59
PARTRIDGE PEA (*Chamaecrista fasciculata*), p. 61
WATER HEMLOCK (*Cicuta maculata*), p. 63
WHITE PRAIRIE CLOVER (*Dalea candida*), p. 65
WHITE PRAIRIE CLOVER (*Dalea purpurea*), p. 67
PRAIRIE-SMOKE (*Geum triflorum*), p. 69
BUSH LESPEDEZA (*Lespedeza capitata*), p. 71
VIRGINIA LESPEDEZA (*Lespedeza virginica*), p. 73
SAMPSON'S SNAKEROOT (*Orbexilum psoralioides*), p. 75
SCURF PEA (*Pediomelum tenuiflorum*), p. 77
PRAIRIE PARSLEY (*Polytaenia nuttallii*), p. 79
PASQUE-FLOWER (*Pulsatilla patens*), p. 81
DROOPING CONEFLOWER (*Ratibida pinnata*), p. 83
CAROLINA ROSE (*Rosa carolina*), p. 85
GOAT'S-RUE (*Tephrosia virginiana*), p. 87
AMERICAN VETCH (*Vicia americana*), p. 89
GOLDEN ALEXANDERS (*Zizia aurea*), p. 91

LEADPLANT
Amorpha canescens Pursh

LEADPLANT

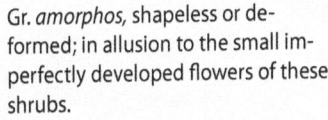

Amorpha canescens Pursh

Family Fabaceae, or Pea Family

Gr. *amorphos*, shapeless or deformed; in allusion to the small imperfectly developed flowers of these shrubs.

Season and Stature Also known as Prairie Shoestring because of its deep roots which may penetrate the soil to depths of fifteen feet or more. The name Leadplant is given because of the plant's lead-gray foliage. It is a warm-season or Summer perennial, and somewhat shrubby. Leadplant reaches a height of about 80 to 100 cm.

Flowers Small, medium to dark purple, and densely aggregated in the racemose inflorescence.

Leaves The lead-gray leaves are pinnately compound with some 21 to 51 leaflets, these covered with fine, gray hairs. Each leaflet is sessile and up to 1 cm wide.

Use or Importance A common upland prairie herb, and closely associated throughout the prairies with the bluestem grasses. The plant is highly nutritious and palatable, and therefore decreases under heavy grazing. Hand-collected seeds can be germinated by weakening the seed coat (scarification). Leadplant is an important species in prairie restorations.

Habitat Sand prairies, gravel-hill prairies.

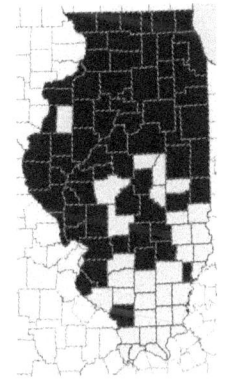

Distribution in Illinois

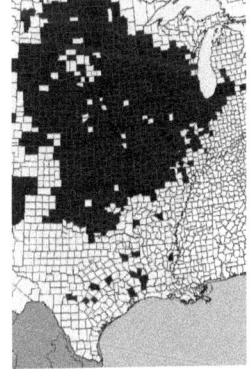

Distribution in central USA

Group B. At least some of the leaves compound, divided into 3 or more distinct segments or leaflets.

CANADIAN ANEMONE
Anemone canadensis L.

CANADIAN ANEMONE
Anemone canadensis L.

Family Ranunculaceae, or Buttercup Family

In Greek mythology, *Anemone* was the name of the daughter of the winds.

Season and Stature Canadian Anemone is a native, cool-season perennial which attains a height up to 60 cm. It flowers during May and into the summer.

Flowers The flower is 2.5 to 3.5 cm wide. There are 5 white perianth parts and numerous stamens and pistils. The flowers are generally not long lasting.

Leaves The basal leaves are long-petioled, wider than long, 3- to 5-parted, and coarsely toothed. The veins are prominently netted. The upper leaves are sessile.

Use or Importance All anemones are attractive plants.

Habitat Moist soils of woods and prairies.

Distribution in Illinois

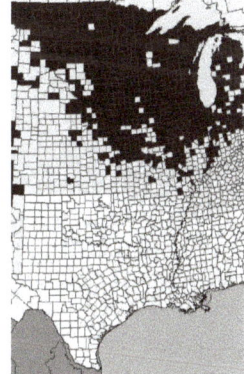

Distribution in central USA

Group B. At least some of the leaves compound, divided into 3 or more distinct segments or leaflets.

CAROLINA ANEMONE
Anemone caroliniana Walt.

CAROLINA ANEMONE

Anemone caroliniana Walt.

In Greek mythology, *Anemone* was the name of the daughter of the winds.

Family Ranunculaceae, or Buttercup Family

Season and Stature Carolina Anemone is a native, cool-season perennial. It grows to a height of 25 cm. Flowering is during Spring.

Flowers The flowers, which are up to 2 cm across, are white to purplish. The perianth parts vary from 6 to 20.

Leaves The basal leaves are slender, petioled, and divided into three divisions which are toothed or lobed. The leaves which subtend the flower are sessile and 3-cleft.

Use or Importance All members of the genus Anemone are beautiful and a delight to the eye.

Habitat Dry, open places. In Illinois, occurs in gravel prairies, loess hill prairies, roadsides, and other dry places.

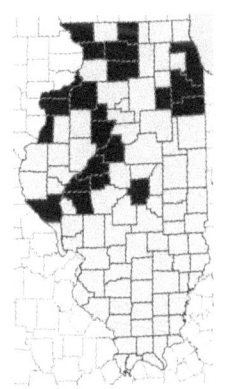
Distribution in Illinois

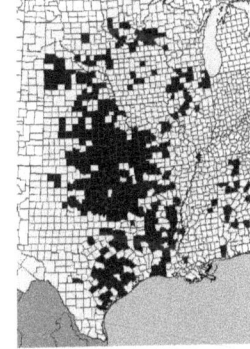
Distribution in central USA

Group B. At least some of the leaves compound, divided into 3 or more distinct segments or leaflets.

WHITE FALSE INDIGO
Baptisia alba (L.) Vent.

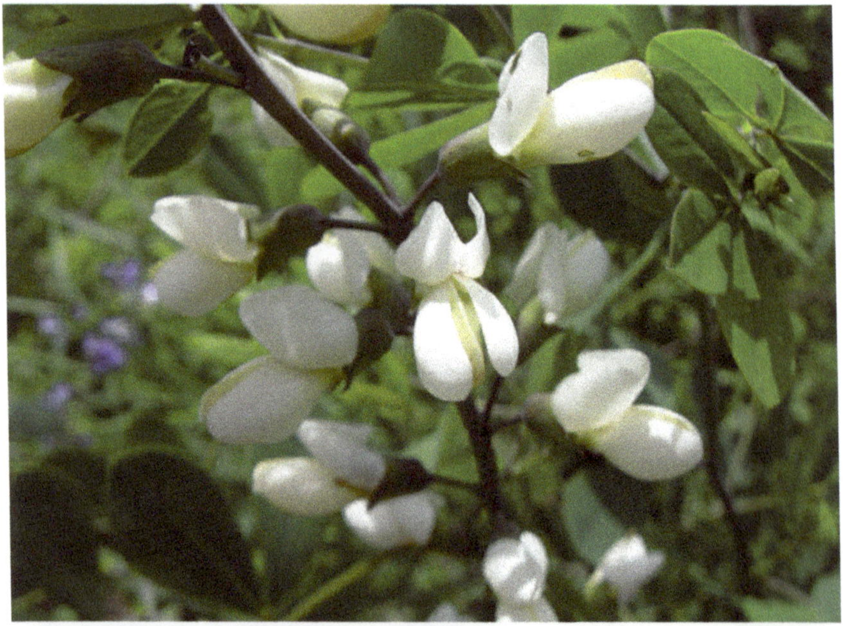

WHITE FALSE INDIGO
Baptisia alba (L.) Vent.

From Gr. *bapto,* to dye. It has sometimes been used as a substitute for true indigo.

Synonym *Baptisia leucantha* Torr. & Gray

Family Fabaceae, or Pea Family

Season and Stature White False Indigo is a native, warm-season perennial. It grows to a height up to 1 meter, and flowers during the Summer.

Flowers The racemes are about 30 cm long and loosely flowered. Each flower is about 1 cm long and white. The flower is typically pea-shaped.

Leaves The leaves are smooth, petioled, trifoliolate, becoming black upon drying. The leaflets are obovate, 1 to 2 cm long, about half as wide as long.

Use or Importance White False Indigo produces a dye used for indigo color. Both the leaves and the fruits are boiled or steeped to obtain this color. The plant behaves as a decreaser when prairie is grazed, but when mature, animals tend to avoid this plant.

Habitat Prairies and woods.

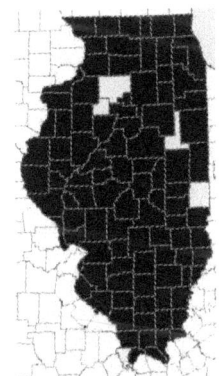
Distribution in Illinois

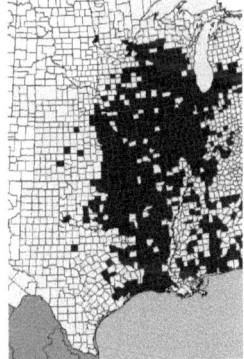
Distribution in central USA

Group B. At least some of the leaves compound, divided into 3 or more distinct segments or leaflets.

WILD FALSE INDIGO
Baptisia bracteata Muhl. ex Ell.

WILD FALSE INDIGO

Baptisia bracteata Muhl. ex Ell.

From Gr. *bapto*, to dye. It has sometimes been used as a substitute for true indigo.

Synonym *Baptisia leucophaea* Nutt.

Family Fabaceae, or Pea Family

Season and Stature This robust herb flowers during the Spring, and grows to a height of 40 to 50 cm.

Flowers The cream-colored, pea-shaped flowers are numerous along mostly horizontally extended racemes at the top of the plant. Each flower may be up to 3 cm long.

Leaves Leaflets are three in number and turn a blue-black color with the first frost. At season's end the plant detaches from the ground, but the leaves remain on the stem.

Use or Importance A dye material of dark blue color has been extracted from the leaves and the fruits. This dye, however, is inferior to the real indigo dye. The plant is not important in providing forage. It is seldom selected for grazing, but does decrease under long grazing use of the prairie. Wild False Indigo is apparently toxic, but affects grazing animals only if eaten in quantity.

Habitat Prairies, open woodlands.

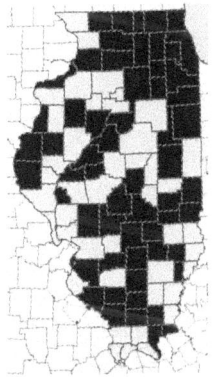
Distribution in Illinois

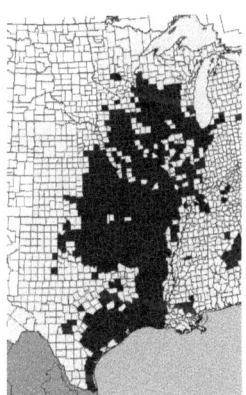
Distribution in central USA

Group B. At least some of the leaves compound, divided into 3 or more distinct segments or leaflets.

PARTRIDGE PEA
Chamaecrista fasciculata (Michx.) Greene

PARTRIDGE PEA   B

Chamaecrista fasciculata (Michx.) Greene

Synonym *Cassia fasciculata* Michx.

Family Fabaceae, or Pea Family

Cassia was the Greek name for a genus of leguminous plants which provide the senna leaves and pods that are important in pharmacy.

Season and Stature This native plant is an annual and is one of a very small number of annual species found in prairie vegetation. It flowers during the Summer and well into Autumn. The height of Partridge Pea is up to 60 cm (or more).

Flowers Showy, yellow, 2.5 to 3.5 cm wide. The flowers are not the typical pea-shape of most legumes, but are almost symmetrical in appearance.

Leaves Pinnately compound with from 12-30 leaflets. The leaflets are linear to narrowly oblong and asymmetrical at the base.

Use or Importance Partridge Pea is very palatable to livestock. It does not rate high as a forage source because it is an annual species. In the south, the plant provides nectar to bees, and is a good honey plant. Partridge Pea tends to grow in infertile places where other plants are sparse, and it improves the soil by its nitrogen-fixing habit. It can be successfully grown from seed by scarification. It is reported to be a good food source for upland birds.

Habitat Sandy soils; particularly common along roads and in old fields.

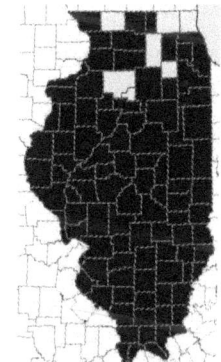
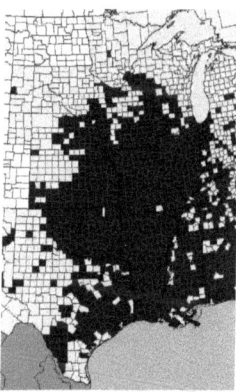

Distribution in Illinois   *Distribution in central USA*

Group B. At least some of the leaves compound, divided into 3 or more distinct segments or leaflets.   61

WATER HEMLOCK
Cicuta maculata L.

WATER HEMLOCK
Cicuta maculata L.

The Latin name for poison hemlock (*Conium maculatum*).

Family Apiaceae, or Carrot Family

Season and Stature Water Hemlock is a native, warm-season perennial. It attains a height up to 1.5 meters. It flowers during Summer.

Flowers The small white flowers are borne in compound, many rayed umbels. Each flower has five sepals, five petals, and five stamens.

Leaves Pinnately compound, arranged alternately on stout, hollow stems. The leaflets are coarsely toothed.

Use or Importance Water Hemlock is poisonous to all warm-blooded animals. The roots and rootstocks are most poisonous. Only a small part of the rootstock, if eaten, is enough to cause death in humans. The poisonous material is cicutoxin; the symptoms of poisoning are frothing, tremoring, and convulsion.

Habitat This species grows in moist situations, including wet prairies.

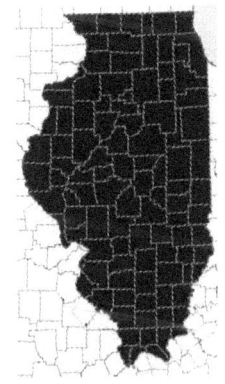

Distribution in Illinois   *Distribution in central USA*

Group B. At least some of the leaves compound, divided into 3 or more distinct segments or leaflets.

WHITE PRAIRIE CLOVER
Dalea candida Michx. ex. Willd.

WHITE PRAIRIE CLOVER

B

Dalea candida Michx. ex. Willd.

In honor of Dr. Samuel Dale (1659-1739), English botanist and author.

Synonym *Petalostemum candidus* Michx.

Family Fabaceae, or Pea Family

Season and Stature White Prairie Clover is a native, warm-season perennial. It attains a height of 30 to 60 cm and blooms during the Summer.

Flowers Numerous small flowers, densely arranged in short spikes. The spikes are 2.5 to 10 cm long and up to 6 mm thick. Each of the white flowers has four petals which are similar, and one which is different in size and shape.

Leaves Pinnately compound with 5-7 leaflets. The leaflets are linear-lanceolate to oblong, up to 3 cm long, and to 4 mm wide.

Use or Importance White Prairie Clover is palatable to grazing animals and decreases when the prairie is grazed.

Habitat Many types of prairies.

Distribution in Illinois

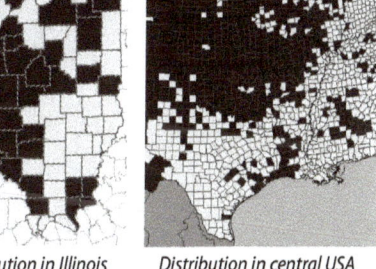

Distribution in central USA

Group B. At least some of the leaves compound, divided into 3 or more distinct segments or leaflets.

PURPLE PRAIRIE CLOVER
Dalea purpurea Vent.

PURPLE PRAIRIE CLOVER

Dalea purpurea Vent.

In honor of Dr. Samuel Dale (1659-1739), English botanist and author.

Synonym *Petalostemum purpureus* (Vent.) Rydb.

Family Fabaceae, or Pea Family

Season and Stature This handsome plant is a native, warm-season herb which grows to a height of 30 to 90 cm. Several stems may grow from a single base.

Flowers Pinkish-purple on elongated spikes 2 to 4 cm long.

Leaves The leaves are divided into 3 to 5 narrow leaflets which may be sparingly hairy.

Use or Importance This plant is highly palatable and nutritious. It is grazed often and tends to decrease under heavy use. Purple Prairie Clover fixes nitrogen in the soil. It has been reported that tea made from the leaves of this plant has a binding or constipating effect. This plant usually ranks high in abundance among native legumes in the prairie.

Habitat Most abundant on uplands of the True Prairie. It also occurs in sand prairies, hill prairies, and gravel-hill prairies.

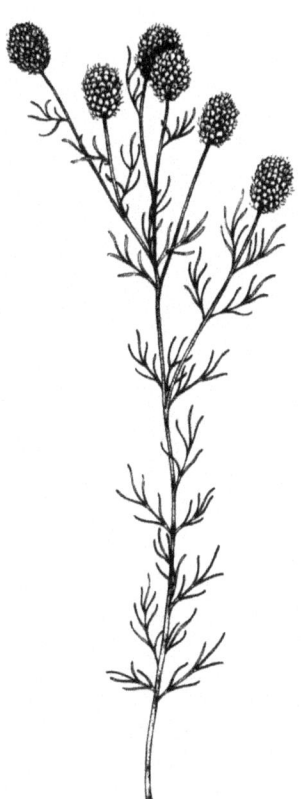

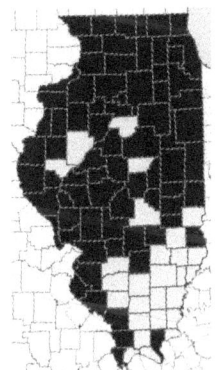

Distribution in Illinois

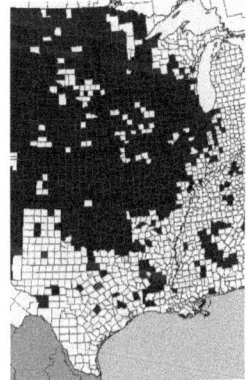

Distribution in central USA

Group B. At least some of the leaves compound, divided into 3 or more distinct segments or leaflets.

PRAIRIE-SMOKE
Geum triflorum Pursh

PRAIRIE-SMOKE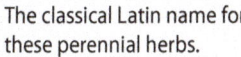
Geum triflorum Pursh

The classical Latin name for these perennial herbs.

Family Rosaceae, or Rose Family

Season and Stature Prairie-smoke is a native cool-season plant. It grows to a height of 15 to 45 cm, and blooms from May through June (late Spring).

Flowers Three flowers are normally borne at the summit of a simple scape. Flowers are up to 1 cm wide, showy, and purple. The fruits are plumose.

Leaves Basal leaves are tufted, petioled, interruptedly pinnate (with small leaflets interspersed among the numerous larger leaflets); stems are softly hairy.

Use or Importance Prairie-smoke is an early-blooming species of unusual appearance. Because of its plumose fruits, it is also called "old man's whiskers."

Habitat Dry, gravelly, or morainal areas; also on calcareous soils in northern Illinois.

  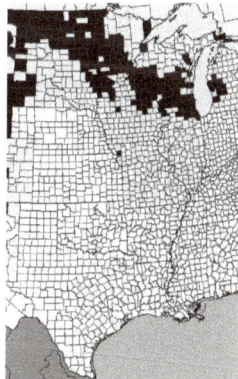

Distribution in Illinois   *Distribution in central USA*

Group B. At least some of the leaves compound, divided into 3 or more distinct segments or leaflets.

BUSH LESPEDEZA
Lespedeza capitata Michx.

BUSH LESPEDEZA
Lespedeza capitata Michx.

Family Fabaceae, or Pea Family

Season and Stature Bush Lespedeza is a native, warm-season perennial. It attains a height of one meter or more. It flowers in late Summer or early Fall.

Flowers The small pea-shaped flowers are borne in a roundish head-like inflorescence which turns a dark brown at maturity. The "heads" are up to 3 cm broad.

Leaves The leaves are divided into three leaflets. The leaflets are elliptical and sometimes covered with fine, silvery hairs.

Use or Importance Bush Lespedeza is an excellent forage plant and behaves as a decreaser under heavy grazing. The seeds of this species, as with many of the lespedezas, provide excellent food for game birds.

Habitat Dry soil of prairies and woods.

Named by the French botanist Michaux (who collected widely in North America) to honor the Spanish governor of Florida, Lespedez, c. 1790.

Distribution in Illinois

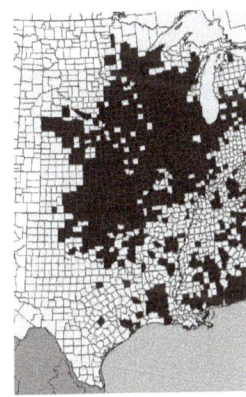
Distribution in central USA

Group B. At least some of the leaves compound, divided into 3 or more distinct segments or leaflets.

VIRGINIA LESPEDEZA
Lespedeza virginica (L.) Britt.

VIRGINIA LESPEDEZA

Lespedeza virginica (L.) Britt.

Family Fabaceae, or Pea Family

Season and Stature This species of *Lespedeza* is a native, warm-season plant. It has slender, erect stems which grow to a height of 1 meter. Flowering during August and September.

Flowers The flowers appear in small clusters on the upper half of the plant; they are small and pinkish colored.

Leaves Compound with three linear or narrowly oblong leaflets. The leaflets are up to 4 cm long and to 7 mm wide.

Use or Importance Virginia Lespedeza is palatable and nutritious and readily grazed. It decreases under heavy grazing. Abundant seeds are produced and supply important food to upland game birds. The seeds germinate without special treatment, and it is therefore not difficult to establish the species in new locations.

Habitat Dry open woods, prairies; tolerant of shade and grows well on clay-loam soils.

Named by the French botanist Michaux (who collected widely in North America) to honor the Spanish governor of Florida, Lespedez, c. 1790.

Distribution in Illinois

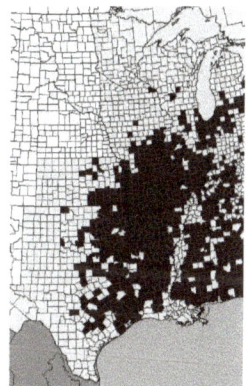

Distribution in central USA

Group B. At least some of the leaves compound, divided into 3 or more distinct segments or leaflets.

SAMPSON'S SNAKEROOT
Orbexilum pedunculatum (P. Mill.) Rydb.

SAMPSON'S SNAKEROOT

Orbexilum pedunculatum (P. Mill.) Rydb.

Psoralea: Gr. *psoraleos*, scabby. Herbs and shrubs sometimes covered with spots.

Synonym *Psoralea psoralioides* (Walt.) Cory

Family Fabaceae, or Pea Family

Season and Stature Sampson's Snakeroot is a cool-season perennial. It attains a height of 30 to 60 cm and blooms during the late Spring. Illinois plants belong to var. *eglandulosum* (Ell.) Isely.

Flowers The flowers are lavender and borne in a dense, spike-like raceme 2.5 to 10 cm long. The flower stalks are much longer than the leaves.

Leaves The 3 leaflets of each leaf are up to 6 cm long. The middle leaflet is on a longer stalk than the others.

Use or Importance This species is grazed and tends to disappear under heavy grazing.

Habitat Rocky glades and prairies of southern Illinois.

Distribution in Illinois

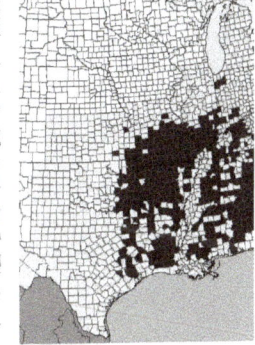

Distribution in central USA

Group B. At least some of the leaves compound, divided into 3 or more distinct segments or leaflets.

SCURF PEA
Pediomelum tenuiflorum (Pursch) A.N. Egan

SCURF PEA

Pediomelum tenuiflorum (Pursch) A.N. Egan

Synonym *Psoralea tenuiflora* Pursh

Family Fabaceae, or Pea Family

Season and Stature Scurf Pea is a native, warm-season perennial attaining a height up to one meter. It flowers in the early Summer.

Flowers The purplish flowers are about 3 mm long and are borne in racemes up to 6 cm long.

Leaves Palmately compound into 3-5 leaflets. The leaflets are oval or elliptic and up to 1 cm long.

Use or Importance Scurf Pea is a palatable and nutritious plant to grazing animals. It decreases when the prairie is grazed.

Habitat Dry prairies, open woods.

Psoralea: Gr. *psoraleos*, scabby. Herbs and shrubs sometimes covered with spots.

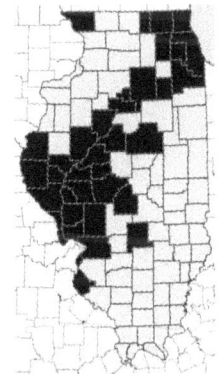
Distribution in Illinois

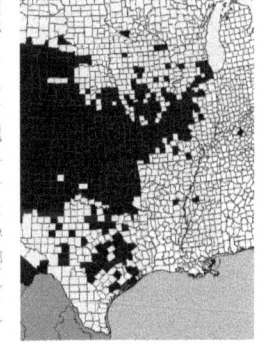
Distribution in central USA

Group B. At least some of the leaves compound, divided into 3 or more distinct segments or leaflets.

PRAIRIE PARSLEY
Polytaenia nuttallii DC.

PRAIRIE PARSLEY
Polytaenia nuttallii DC.

From the greek *polys* (many) and *tainia* (band or ribbon), referring to the many oil tubes.

Family Apiaceae, or Carrot Family

Season and Stature Prairie Parsley is a native, cool-season perennial. It grows to 60 cm tall, and flowers during the Spring.

Flowers The yellow flowers are borne in 6- to 12-rayed umbels. The flower stalks are finely pubescent.

Leaves The leaves are twice pinnately compound. Each leaf segment is deeply pinnatifid with dentate or entire lobes.

Use or Importance Many members of the parsley family are important condiments and seasonings, but wild specimens should never be used, as some members of the Carrot Family are deadly poisonous.

Habitat Dry prairies, open woods.

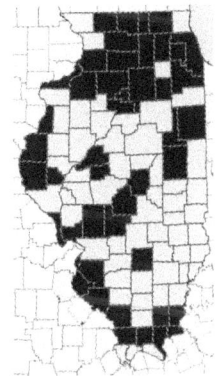

Distribution in Illinois

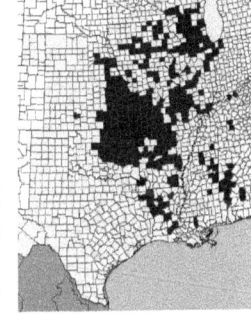

Distribution in central USA

Group B. At least some of the leaves compound, divided into 3 or more distinct segments or leaflets.

PASQUE-FLOWER
Pulsatilla patens (L.) P. Mill.

PASQUE-FLOWER

Pulsatilla patens (L.) P. Mill.

Synonym *Anemone patens* L.

Family Ranunculaceae, or Buttercup Family

Season and Stature Pasque-flower is a native, cool-season perennial herb which attains a height up to 20 cm. It flowers during Spring.

Flowers and Fruits The perianth is light bluish-purple. The perianth segments are ovate-oblong. Fruits are clustered in a dense head of silky achenes with long plumose styles.

Leaves The leaves are dissected into linear lobes. The basal leaves are on slender petioles, while the leaves of the upper stem are sessile. The entire plant has a covering of soft hairs.

Use or Importance In the northern prairies, Pasque-flower was eagerly looked for in flower and was regarded as a sign that Spring was at hand.

Habitat In Illinois, this plant occurs in the gravel and hill prairies in the northern tier of counties.

In Greek mythology, *Anemone* was the name of the daughter of the winds.

Distribution in Illinois

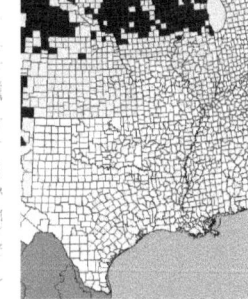

Distribution in central USA

Group B. At least some of the leaves compound, divided into 3 or more distinct segments or leaflets.

DROOPING CONEFLOWER
Ratibida pinnata (Vent.) Barnh.

DROOPING CONEFLOWER

B

Ratibida pinnata (Vent.) Barnh.

Family Asteraceae, or Aster Family

Season and Stature Drooping Coneflower is sometimes also called Weary Susan or the Gray-headed Coneflower. It is a native, warm-season, tall perennial which attains a height of about 1 m. It flowers from June to September.

Flowers The flowers are grouped in a head. The rays, which are yellow and turned downward, number from 4 to 10. The rays are 2.5 to 7 cm long and to nearly 1 cm wide. The disk is gray-green and twice as tall as thick.

Leaves The lower leaves are pinnately 3 to 7 parted, with the segments lanceolate, dentate, cleft, or entire. They are petiolate. The upper leaves are sessile or nearly so. All leaves are very smooth.

Use or Importance Drooping Coneflower decreases when the prairie is overgrazed. It is attractive to grazing animals in its young growth.

Habitat Many types of moist to drier prairie situations.

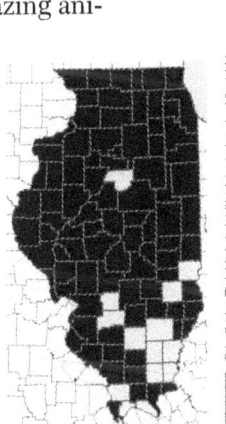
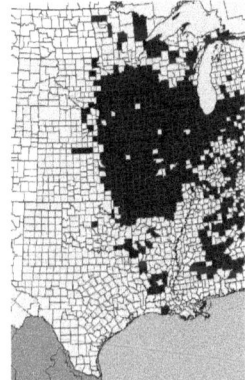

Distribution in Illinois   *Distribution in central USA*

Group B. At least some of the leaves compound, divided into 3 or more distinct segments or leaflets.

CAROLINA ROSE
Rosa carolina L.

CAROLINA ROSE   B

Rosa carolina L. The Latin name.

Family Rosaceae, or Rose Family

Season and Stature Carolina Rose is a native, warm-season perennial herb attaining a height of up to 90 cm. It flowers during the Summer.

Flowers The pale pink flowers are usually solitary on the branches. Each flower is 3 to 5 cm wide. The fruit is about 0.5 cm long.

Leaves Pinnately compound, composed of 5 to 9 leaflets. The leaflets are usually elliptic and up to 4 cm long; they are conspicuously toothed. The stems which bear the leaves are sparsely prickly.

Use or Importance The fruits, called rose hips, are rich in Vitamin C. These hips may be used to make jelly.

Habitat Dry, sandy, rocky, or clay soils in sparse woods, open fields, and prairies.

Distribution in Illinois

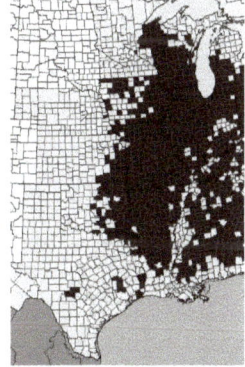

Distribution in central USA

Group B. At least some of the leaves compound, divided into 3 or more distinct segments or leaflets.

GOAT'S-RUE
Tephrosia virginiana (L.) Pers.

GOAT'S-RUE

Tephrosia virginiana (L.) Pers. — Gr. *tephros*, ash-colored; from the appearance of the leaves of these perennial herbs.

Family Fabaceae, or Pea Family

Season and Stature Goat's-rue is a native, warm-season perennial. It grows from several stems and reaches a height of 30 to 60 cm. It flowers during the Summer.

Flowers The large flowers are up to 2 cm long and borne in terminal racemes. The flowers are multi-colored, in tints of cream, pink, and purple. The petals are the typical shape found in the pea family.

Leaves Pinnately compound, with the 15-31 leaflets tapering at each end and silky-hairy.

Use or Importance A nutritious, palatable plant which is relished by livestock of all kinds. It decreases in prairies where grazing is heavy. The plant is considered a sensitive indicator of the condition of prairie rangeland.

Habitat This handsome herb is found in hill prairies and sand prairies and on a wide variety of upland sites.

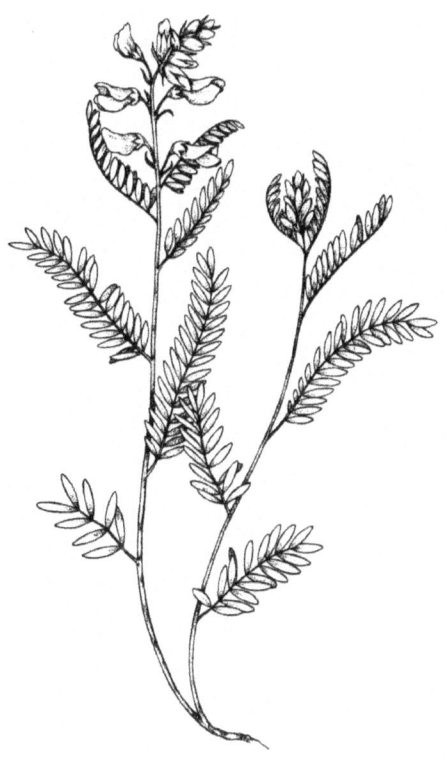

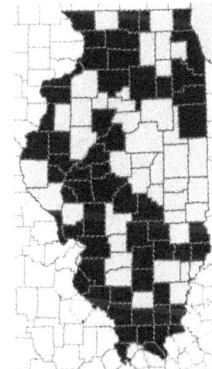
Distribution in Illinois

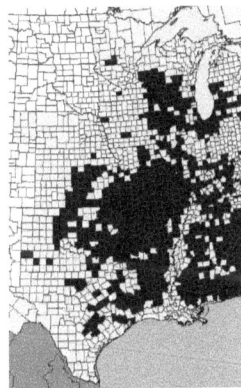
Distribution in central USA

Group B. At least some of the leaves compound, divided into 3 or more distinct segments or leaflets.

AMERICAN VETCH
Vicia americana Muhl. ex Willd.

AMERICAN VETCH

Vicia americana Muhl. ex Willd.

The Latin name for these herbs.

Family Fabaceae, or Pea Family

Season and Stature American Vetch is a perennial, warm-season herb with a trailing habit, growing to about 90 cm long. It blooms during the late-Spring and Summer.

Flowers The inflorescence is a 3- to 9-flowered raceme. The bluish-purple flowers are about 1 cm long and typically pea shaped.

Leaves The leaflets of the compound leaves are 8 to 18 in number, elliptical, sharply toothed, and 1 to 2 cm long.

Use or Importance Palatable forage for livestock is provided by the American Vetch. It is also often seeded along highways or near road shoulders or cuts to help stabilize the soil; it forms a good cover in such situations.

Habitat Prairies, often where somewhat disturbed.

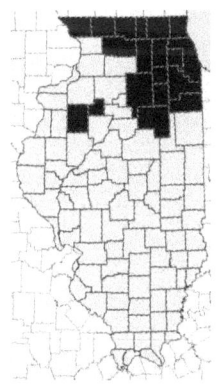
Distribution in Illinois

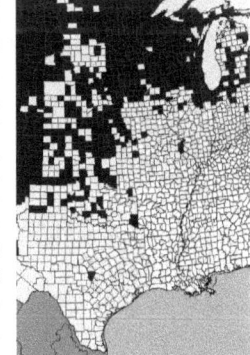
Distribution in central USA

Group B. At least some of the leaves compound, divided into 3 or more distinct segments or leaflets.

GOLDEN ALEXANDERS
Zizia aurea (L.) W.D.J. Koch

GOLDEN ALEXANDERS

Zizia aurea (L.) W.D.J. Koch

Named for J.B. Ziz, 19th century German botanist.

Family Apiaceae, or Carrot Family

Season and Stature Golden Alexanders is also known as the Golden Meadow Parsnip. It is a native, cool-season perennial. It grows to about 75 cm tall, and blooms in late-Spring.

Flowers The golden yellow flowers are small and borne in umbels having 9 to 25 short, ascending rays; the rays up to 5 cm long.

Leaves The basal leaves are long petioled, 2 to 3 ternately compound, and sharply serrate.

Use or Importance *Zizia* is an important plant to a number of insects that are able to easily reach the nectar in the small yellow flowers. Black Swallowtail caterpillars feed on its leaves.

Habitat Moist habitats, including prairies and woods.

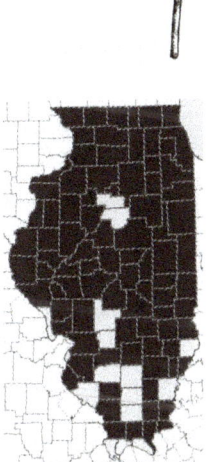

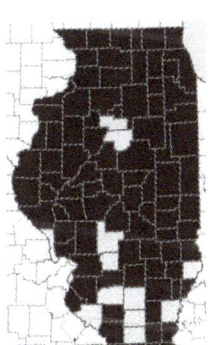

Distribution in Illinois   *Distribution in central USA*

Group B. At least some of the leaves compound, divided into 3 or more distinct segments or leaflets.

GROUP C

Leaves of **Rosinweed** (*Silphium integrifolium*), see p. 135.

GROUP C

Leaves simple, opposite or whorled.

Hairy Green Milkweed (*Asclepias hirtella*), p. 95
Sullivant's Milkweed (*Asclepias sullivantii*), p. 97
Whorled Milkweed (*Asclepias verticillata*), p. 99
Green Milkweed (*Asclepias viridiflora*), p. 101
Blue Hearts (*Buchnera americana*), p. 103
Stiff Tickseed (*Coreopsis palmata*), p. 105
Stiff Marsh Bedstraw (*Galium tinctorium*), p. 107
Closed Gentian (*Gentiana andrewsii*), p. 109
Downy Gentian (*Gentiana puberulenta*), p. 111
Stiff Sunflower (*Helianthus pauciflorus*), p. 113
Sawtooth Sunflower (*Helianthus grosseserratus*), p. 115
Hairy Sunflower (*Helianthus mollis*), p. 117
Jerusalem Artichoke (*Helianthus tuberosus*), p. 119
False Sunflower (*Heliopsis helianthoides*), p. 121
Fringed Loosestrife (*Lysimachia ciliata*), p. 123
Wild Bergamot (*Monarda fistulosa*), p. 125
Prairie Phlox (*Phlox pilosa*), p. 127
Mountain Mint (*Pycnanthemum tenuifolium*), p. 129
Prairie Hyssop (*Pycnanthemum virginianum*), p. 131
Wild Petunia (*Ruellia humilis*), p. 133
Rosinweed (*Silphium integrifolium*), p. 135
Cup-plant (*Silphium perfoliatum*), p. 137
American Germander (*Teucrium canadense*), p. 139
Culver's-root (*Veronicastrum virginicum*), p. 141

HAIRY GREEN MILKWEED
Asclepias hirtella (Pennell) Woods.

HAIRY GREEN MILKWEED

Asclepias hirtella (Pennell) Woods. The Greek name for these plants, in honor of Asclepias, god of medicine.

Family Asclepiadaceae, or Milkweed Family

Season and Stature Hairy Green Milkweed is a native, warm-season perennial which may grow to a height of one meter. It flowers during the Summer.

Flowers Hairy Green Milkweed has the typical hour-glass shaped flowers of milkweeds. Several greenish flowers are borne in groups from the axils of the leaves.

Leaves The alternate or opposite leaves are linear to linear-lanceolate and rough to the touch. There is latex present.

Use or Importance This milkweed is known for producing many flowers. It is attractive to butterflies and bees, mostly notably honeybees, bumblebees, and leaf-cutting bees.

Habitat Dry prairies.

Distribution in Illinois

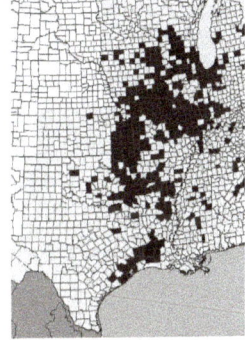

Distribution in central USA

Group C. Leaves simple, opposite or whorled

SULLIVANT'S MILKWEED
Asclepias sullivantii Engelm. ex Gray

SULLIVANT'S MILKWEED

Asclepias sullivantii Engelm. ex Gray

The Greek name for these plants, in honor of Asclepias, god of medicine.

Family Asclepiadaceae, or Milkweed Family

Season and Stature Sullivant's Milkweed is a native, warm-season perennial. It may attain a height slightly over 1 meter. It flowers from July to September.

Flowers The umbels are wide-spreading, mostly terminal, or sometimes in the upper axils. The purplish flowers are about 1 cm long.

Leaves The thick leaves are sessile or on short petioles. They are oblong or ovate-oblong, with a mucronate tip. The veins are conspicuous and pinnate.

Use or Importance Visited by hummingbirds and a wide variety of bees and butterflies (including Monarchs). Prairie Milkweed is one of the plants favored by the larvae of the Milkweed Leaf-Miner fly, which bore holes in the leaves.

Habitat Moist prairies.

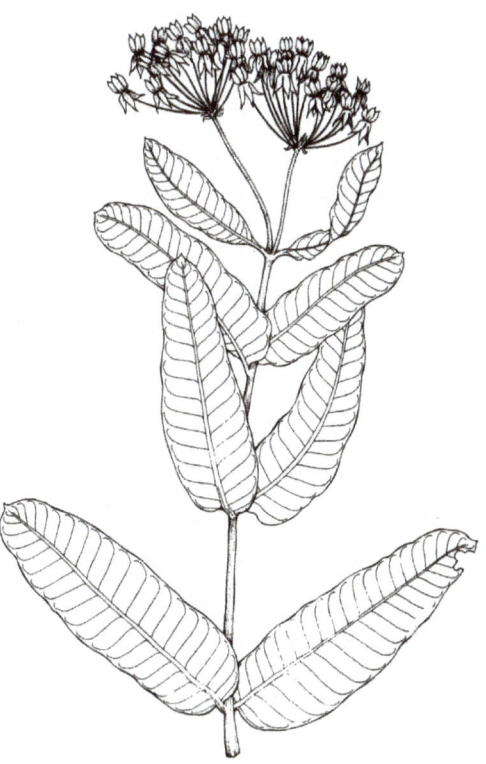

Distribution in Illinois

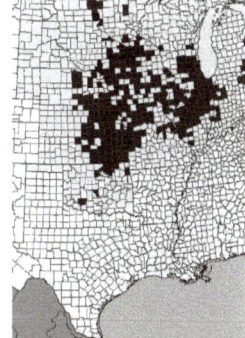
Distribution in central USA

Group C. Leaves simple, opposite or whorled

WHORLED MILKWEED
Asclepias verticillata L.

WHORLED MILKWEED
Asclepias verticillata L.

The Greek name for these plants, in honor of Asclepias, god of medicine.

Family Asclepiadaceae, or Milkweed Family

Season and Stature Whorled Milkweed is a native, warm-season perennial plant, and attains a height of up to 60 cm. Plants have rhizomes and will spread to form colonies. It flowers during the late Summer and Fall.

Flowers The flowers are greenish-white, borne on many-flowered umbels on slender pedicels. The umbels are numerous. Flowers have the typical hour-glass shape of the milkweed family.

Leaves Linear and sessile, and arranged in verticillate or whorled clusters of 3 to 7. The margins of the leaves may be slightly rolled or involute.

Use or Importance The nectar of the flowers attracts many kinds of insects, including long-tongued bees, short-tongued bees, wasps, flies, butterflies, skippers, and beetles.

Habitat Whorled Milkweed is found in dry prairies, on hills, and in fields. In Illinois, it occurs in all types of dry prairie.

Distribution in Illinois

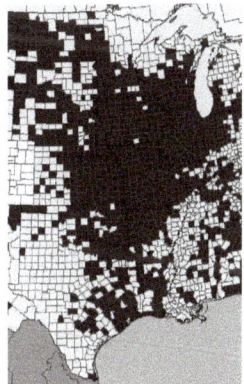

Distribution in central USA

GREEN MILKWEED
Asclepias viridiflora Raf.

GREEN MILKWEED

Asclepias viridiflora Raf.

The Greek name for these plants, in honor of Asclepias, god of medicine.

Synonym *Acerates viridiflora* (Raf.) Pursh ex Eat.

Family Asclepiadaceae, or Milkweed Family

Season and Stature Green Milkweed is a native, warm-season, perennial herb attaining a height of 30 to 90 cm. It flowers during June to September.

Flowers The flowers are borne in dense terminal and axillary umbels. Pedicels are 4 to 8 mm long. The flowers are green and have an hour-glass shape. This shape is typical for milkweed flowers and is due to a structure on the flower known as a corona.

Leaves The leaves are slightly rough to touch, alternate or opposite, oval, oblong, or ovate to lanceolate. Leaves are 2.5 to 12 cm long and up to 4 cm wide. They have short petioles.

Use or Importance The flowers attract bumblebees and other long-tongued bees, which are the most common pollinators.

Habitat In Illinois, Green Milkweed is found in dry upland prairies, hill prairies, and sand prairies.

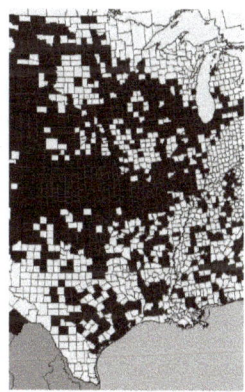

Distribution in Illinois   Distribution in central USA

Group C. Leaves simple, opposite or whorled

BLUE HEARTS
Buchnera americana L.

BLUE HEARTS
Buchnera americana L.

Family Orobanchaceae, or Broom-Rape Family

Season and Stature Blue Hearts is a native, warm-season perennial herb. It attains a height of 30 to 75 cm. It blooms during the Summer.

Flowers The inflorescence is a spike. The flowers are light to medium purple in color. They are nearly regular, about 1 cm long,w and nearly as ide.

Leaves The leaves are opposite. The lower leaves are obovate to oblong and obtuse; the middle leaves are oblong-lanceolate, dentate, and narrowed to the sessile base. The upper leaves are linear-lanceolate and entire or nearly so.

Use or Importance Although there is no particular importance for this plant, it adds a lovely color to the prairie landscape during the summer.

Habitat In Illinois, this species is found mostly in hill prairies. It is not common. Elsewhere, *Buchnera* occurs in sandy, gravelly, or dry loess soil over the eastern half of the United States, including southern portions of the True Prairie area.

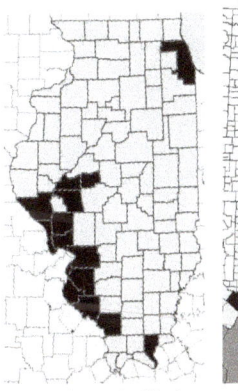
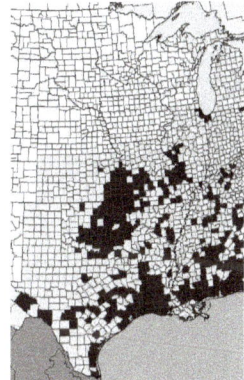

Distribution in Illinois   Distribution in central USA

Group C. Leaves simple, opposite or whorled

STIFF TICKSEED
Coreopsis palmata Nutt.

STIFF TICKSEED

Coreopsis palmata Nutt.

From Gr. *koris*, a bug; *opsis*, like. The seed of these herbs looks like a bug or tick.

Family Asteraceae, or Aster Family

Season and Stature Stiff Tickseed is a native, warm-season perennial. It attains a height of up to 90 cm and flowers during the Summer.

Flowers The flowers are bright and deep yellow, measuring 2.5 to 5 cm wide. Both disk flowers and ray flowers are present in the heads. The disk flowers are perfect and fertile, while the ray flowers are neutral. The rays are mostly 3-toothed at the tip. The few heads are borne on short peduncles.

Leaves Opposite, sessile, up to 7.5 cm long, and palmately 3-lobed to about the middle; the lobes are linear-oblong.

Use or Importance Because of the deep yellow color of the petals, a dye has been obtained from the flowers; it is most effective on wool.

Habitat Dry prairies, open woods.

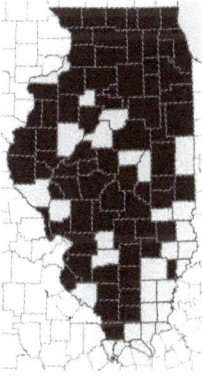
Distribution in Illinois

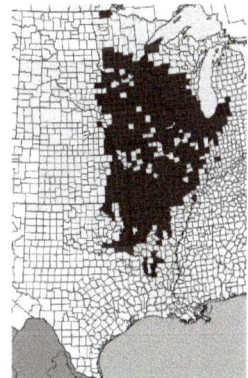
Distribution in central USA

Group C. Leaves simple, opposite or whorled

STIFF MARSH BEDSTRAW
Galium tinctorium (L.) Scop.

STIFF MARSH BEDSTRAW

Galium tinctorium (L.) Scop.

From Gr. *gala*, milk. Yellow bedstraw (*G. verum*) can be used in cheese-making to curdle the milk.

Family Rubiaceae, or Madder Family

Season and Stature Stiff Marsh Bedstraw is a native, warm-season perennial. It grows 15 to 30 cm long, and blooms during early Summer.

Flowers The flowers are in terminal clusters of 2 to 3. The pedicels are slender, bearing white, 4-parted flowers, 1 to 2 mm wide. The ovary is inferior.

Leaves The leaves are in clusters of 4, 5, or 6 along the square stems. The leaves are linear to lanceolate, broadest below the middle, and tapered at each end.

Use or Importance This plant is called bedstraw from the fact that it and other species of the genus were formerly used as stuffing for mattresses or bed ticking. It has also been mixed with rennet in cheese-making.

Habitat In many types of moist habitats, including low prairies.

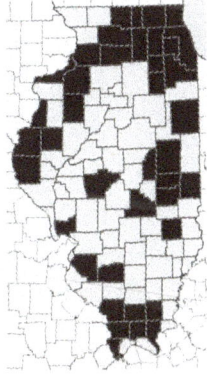
Distribution in Illinois
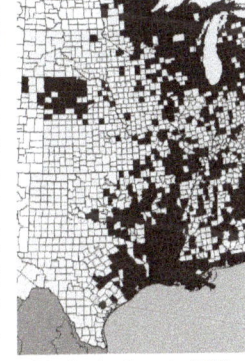
Distribution in central USA

Group C. Leaves simple, opposite or whorled

CLOSED GENTIAN
Gentiana andrewsii Griseb.

CLOSED GENTIAN

Gentiana andrewsii Griseb.

Family Gentianaceae, or Gentian Family

Season and Stature Closed Gentian is a native, warm-season perennial which may grow to a height of 60 cm. It flowers from August to October.

Flowers As the common name indicates, the flowers are closed (or nearly so). The corolla, which is blue or pale bluish, is 2.5 to 3.5 cm long. The flowers are borne either in a terminal cluster of 2 to 4, or in upper axils where there may be 1 to 2.

Leaves Ovate to lanceolate, 3- to 7-nerved, pointed at the tip, somewhat rounded at the base, and sessile.

Use or Importance The bitter juice of the gentians have long been valued as a tonic. This plant has sometimes been called "ague-weed."

Habitat Damp prairies.

Named for King Gentius of Illyria who was reputed to have discovered the medicinal virtues of the root of the yellow gentian or bitterwort (*G. lutea*) from which a tonic bitters is still made.

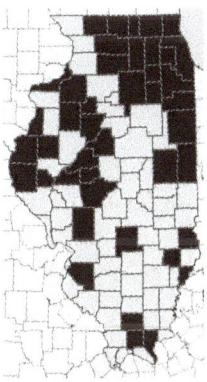
Distribution in Illinois

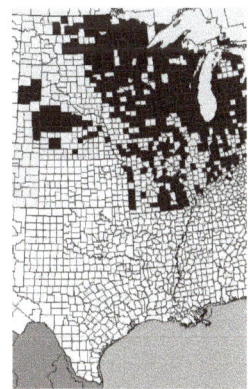
Distribution in central USA

Group C. Leaves simple, opposite or whorled

DOWNY GENTIAN
Gentiana puberulenta J. Pringle

DOWNY GENTIAN

Gentiana puberulenta J. Pringle

Family Gentianaceae, or Gentian Family

Season and Stature This late-blooming gentian of the Gentianaceae family is a native, warm-season or fall-blooming perennial herb. It attains a height of 20 to 40 cm (or more), and blooms from August to October, where it is much over-topped by the grasses at this time.

Flowers Deep blue, tubular, of 5 petals, 5 stamens, and a superior ovary. The flowers are sessile or nearly so in the upper axils of the leaves; flowers are rarely solitary and terminal.

Leaves The stems are usually solitary with lanceolate upper leaves; the lower leaves are slightly oblong. The leaves are narrowed at the base, and from 2.5 to 7.5 cm long.

Use or Importance This species decreases under grazing. The deep blue flower makes it especially attractive.

Habitat Found in most Illinois dry prairie types.

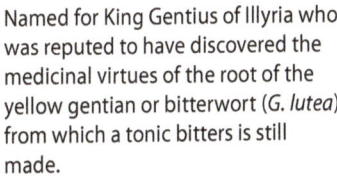

Named for King Gentius of Illyria who was reputed to have discovered the medicinal virtues of the root of the yellow gentian or bitterwort (*G. lutea*) from which a tonic bitters is still made.

Distribution in Illinois

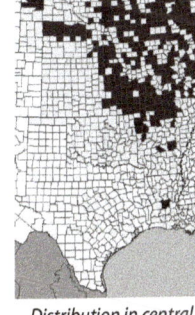

Distribution in central USA

Group C. Leaves simple, opposite or whorled

SAWTOOTH SUNFLOWER
Helianthus grosseserratus Martens

SAWTOOTH SUNFLOWER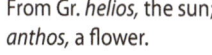

Helianthus grosseserratus Martens

From Gr. *helios*, the sun; *anthos*, a flower.

Family Asteraceae, or Aster Family

Season and Stature Sawtooth Sunflower is a robust, native, warm-season perennial herb, growing to 2.5 meters tall. It flowers during the late-Summer and Fall.

Flowers The ray flowers are neutral; the disk flowers are perfect and fertile. The heads are numerous, 3 to 7 cm wide, with 10 to 20 deep yellow rays. The disk is yellowish.

Leaves Long-lanceolate, with slender petioles. The upper leaves are alternate, the lower ones opposite. Leaves are sharply serrate, rough above, hairy beneath, 10 to 20 cm long, and to 2.5 cm wide.

Use or Importance The presence of this species was formerly used as an indicator of good corn land.

Habitat In Illinois, this species occurs in all parts of the state and probably in every moist to wet prairie type.

Distribution in Illinois

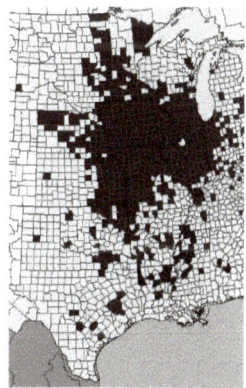
Distribution in central USA

Group C. Leaves simple, opposite or whorled

HAIRY SUNFLOWER
Helianthus mollis Lam.

HAIRY SUNFLOWER
Helianthus mollis Lam.

From Gr. *helios*, the sun; *anthos*, a flower.

Family Asteraceae, or Aster Family

Season and Stature Hairy Sunflower is a warm-season, mid-sized perennial, reaching a height of about one meter. It flowers during the Summer and Fall.

Flowers The flower heads are 5 to 6 cm wide, and bear several yellow rays around a yellow disk.

Leaves Sessile, opposite on the stem. The leaves are densely hairy and rough to the touch.

Use or Importance Hairy Sunflower is highly nutritious and palatable and is relished by grazing animals. For this reason, it decreases under grazing.

Habitat Dry soil in prairies and woods.

Distribution in Illinois

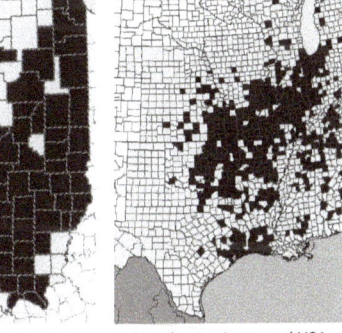

Distribution in central USA

Group C. Leaves simple, opposite or whorled

STIFF SUNFLOWER
Helianthus pauciflorus Nutt.

STIFF SUNFLOWER

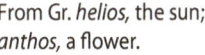

Helianthus pauciflorus Nutt.

From Gr. *helios*, the sun; *anthos*, a flower.

Synonym *Helianthus rigidus* (Cass.) Desf.

Family Asteraceae, or Aster Family

Season and Stature Stiff Sunflower is a warm-season perennial, growing to about 1 meter high; blooming during the late-Summer and Fall.

Flowers The rays of Stiff Sunflower are over 1 cm long and surround the red or purple disk.

Leaves Oppositely arranged, lanceolate to ovate, mostly toothed, rough to the touch on both surfaces.

Use or Importance Stiff Sunflower is palatable to grazing animals, and decreases under grazing pressure.

Habitat Dry prairies.

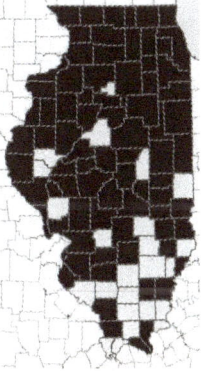

Distribution in Illinois

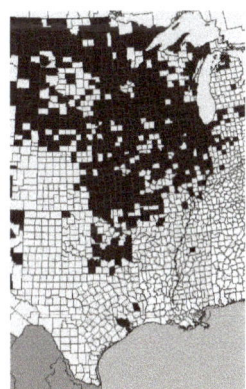

Distribution in central USA

Group C. Leaves simple, opposite or whorled

JERUSALEM ARTICHOKE
Helianthus tuberosus L.

JERUSALEM ARTICHOKE

Helianthus tuberosus L.

From Gr. *helios,* the sun; *anthos,* a flower.

Family Asteraceae, or Aster Family

Season and Stature Jerusalem Artichoke is a native, warm-season perennial, growing to 3 meters tall. It blooms during the Fall.

Flowers There are several yellow heads on each plant, measuring up to 8 cm wide. The rays, which number from 12 to 20, and the disk are yellow.

Leaves Ovate, ovate-oblong, or ovate-lanceolate, 3-veined, narrowed at the base, petiolate, rough to the touch, and serrate. They are up to 20 cm long and to 7 cm wide. The upper leaves are alternate, while the lower ones are generally opposite.

Use or Importance Jerusalem Artichoke has thickened, starchy tubers, which are edible. The plant is adaptable to cultivation and the tubers are available commercially (sometimes under the brand name "Sunchokes."

Habitat Wet prairies, damp woods, roadsides.

Distribution in Illinois

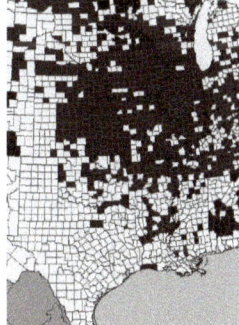

Distribution in central USA

Group C. Leaves simple, opposite or whorled

FALSE SUNFLOWER
Heliopsis helianthoides (L.) Sweet

FALSE SUNFLOWER

Heliopsis helianthoides (L.) Sweet   Gr. *helios*, the sun; *opsis*, resembling. In allusion to the rayed yellow flower heads.

Family Asteraceae, or Aster Family

Season and Stature False Sunflower is a native, warm-season perennial herb. It attains a height of a meter or more and blooms during the Fall.

Flowers The heads are long peduncled, and are 3 to 6 cm broad. The yellow disk flowers bear both stamens and pistils, while the yellow ray flowers have only pistils.

Leaves Opposite, petioled, ovate-lanceolate, acuminate at the tip, sharply toothed, somewhat rough on both surfaces, 7 to 15 cm long, and 2.5 to 6 cm wide.

Use or Importance The plant is palatable to livestock and tends to decrease in prairies which are grazed.

Habitat Open woods and dry prairies.

Distribution in Illinois

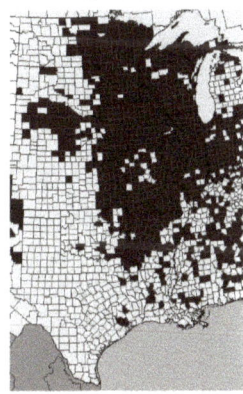

Distribution in central USA

Group C. Leaves simple, opposite or whorled

FRINGED LOOSESTRIFE
Lysimachia ciliata L.

FRINGED LOOSESTRIFE
Lysimachia ciliata L.

So named by Dioscorides after King Lysimachus of Thracia.

Family Primulaceae, or Primrose Family

Season and Stature Fringed Loosestrife is a native, warm-season perennial, growing from 30 cm to nearly 1 meter high. It blooms during the Summer.

Flowers The flowers are pale yellow. There are 5 corolla segments, each up to about 1 cm in length.

Leaves Ovate-oblong or ovate-lanceolate, pinnately veined, acuminate at the apex, cordate at the base. The leaves are 5 to 15 cm long. The lower margins of the leaves and the petioles are finely ciliate, accounting for the common name.

Use or Importance Pliny believed this plant to take away strife between beasts which were yoked together, and to help make them tame.

Habitat Moist prairies, moist woods, low ground.

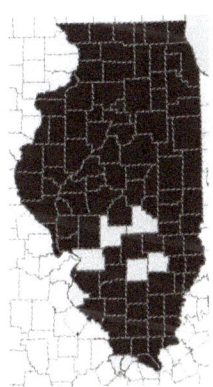
Distribution in Illinois

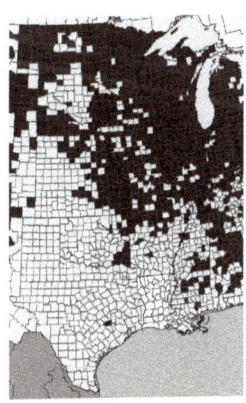
Distribution in central USA

WILD BERGAMOT
Monarda fistulosa L.

WILD BERGAMOT
Monarda fistulosa L.

Family Lamiaceae, or Mint Family

Season and Stature Wild Bergamot is a native, warm-season perennial which blooms during the Summer and Fall. It attains a height of 60 cm or more.

Flowers 2-lipped and purplish or lavender; numerous in a spherical head.

Leaves Ovate-lanceolate, toothed, prominently veined, and arranged oppositely on the square stems.

Use or Importance The plant's flowers are attractive to bees, and is considered a good honey plant. The plant is not important from the standpoint of grazing. Wild Bergamot can be grown in gardens as an ornamental.

Habitat Dry situations in woods and prairies.

Named for Nicholas Monardes (1493-1588), physician and botanist of Seville who wrote a book in 1571 on American products.

Distribution in Illinois

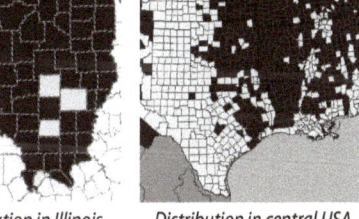

Distribution in central USA

PRAIRIE PHLOX
Phlox pilosa L.

PRAIRIE PHLOX

Phlox pilosa L.

Gr. *phlox*, a flame. Also the Greek name for some plant with flame-colored flowers.

Family Polemoniaceae, or Phlox Family

Season and Stature Prairie Phlox is a cool-season herb. It attains a height of up to 60 cm. Prairie Phlox flowers during the Spring.

Flowers The inflorescence is cymose-corymbose. The flowers are short-pedicelled, and the five petals are fused into a tubular flower which is pink or purple.

Leaves Simple, opposite, linear or lanceolate, 2.5 to 10 cm long, and sessile.

Use or Importance Prairie Phlox has been grown successfully as a garden plant.

Habitat Prairies and dry woods.

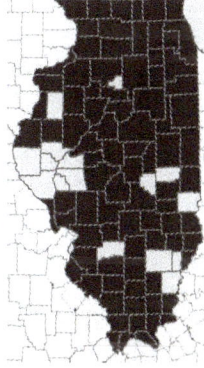

Distribution in Illinois

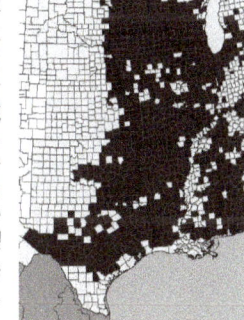

Distribution in central USA

Group C. Leaves simple, opposite or whorled

MOUNTAIN MINT
Pycnanthemum tenuifolium Schrad.

MOUNTAIN MINT

Pycnanthemum tenuifolium Schrad.

Gr. *pyknos,* dense; *anthos,* a flower. The flowers of these perennial herbs are densely arranged.

Family Lamiaceae, or Mint Family

Season and Stature Mountain Mint is a native, warm-season perennial herb which attains a height of about 60 cm. It blooms from July to September.

Flowers The flowers are tubular, 2-lipped, white dotted with purple, and borne in terminal clusters. The upper lip of the flower is entire, while the lower is 3-cleft. The stamens are 4 and about equal in length.

Leaves Linear to lanceolate, entire and smooth; the upper leaves sessile and the lower short-petioled. The leaves are opposite on the square stems and have a mint odor.

Use or Importance A tea is reportedly made from the leaves of this species.

Habitat In a variety of dry and moist habitats including prairies.

Distribution in Illinois

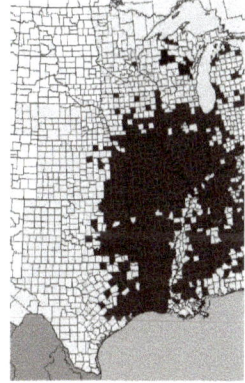

Distribution in central USA

Group C. Leaves simple, opposite or whorled

PRAIRIE HYSSOP

Pycnanthemum virginianum (L.) T. Dur. & B.D. Jackson

PRAIRIE HYSSOP

Pycnanthemum virginianum (L.) T. Dur. & B.D. Jackson

Family Lamiaceae, or Mint Family

Season and Stature A native warm-season perennial. It attains a height of 30 to 90 cm and blooms from July to September.

Flowers The flowers are densely arranged in head-like clusters or glomerules which are about 0.5 cm in diameter. Each flower is small, pubescent, and purple-spotted. The corolla tube is longer than the calyx.

Leaves The leaves are lanceolate, acute at the tip, entire, fragrant, and sessile. Some of the leaves are minutely hairy.

Use or Importance The leaves can be used as seasoning in cooking.

Habitat Dry pastures and gravel hill prairies.

Gr. *pyknos*, dense; *anthos*, a flower. The flowers of these perennial herbs are densely arranged.

Distribution in Illinois

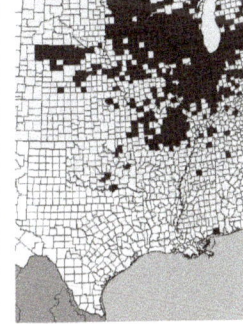
Distribution in central USA

Group C. Leaves simple, opposite or whorled

WILD PETUNIA
Ruellia humilis Nutt.

WILD PETUNIA
Ruellia humilis Nutt.

Herbs and shrubs named for Jean de la Ruelle (1474-1537), herbalist to Francois I of France.

Family Acanthaceae, or Acanthus Family

Season and Stature Wild Petunia is a native, warm-season perennial. It attains a height up to 70 cm, and blooms during the Summer and Fall.

Flowers The flowers are purple to pale purple or blue and clustered or solitary in the axils of the leaves. The corolla is composed of 5 fused petals to make a tube-like, petunia-shaped flower. The flower is up to 3 cm wide and from 3 to 5 cm long.

Leaves Hairy, oval or ovate, sessile, and from 3.5 to 7 cm long.

Use or Importance Some members of the genus *Ruellia* have been used as sources of dyes and of drugs.

Habitat A variety of dry habitats, including prairies and woods.

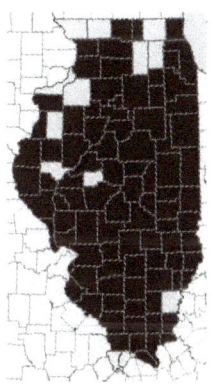
Distribution in Illinois

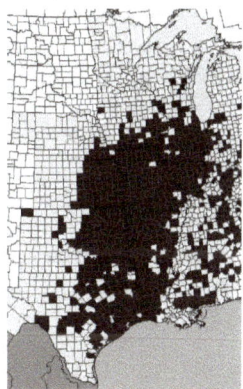
Distribution in central USA

Group C. Leaves simple, opposite or whorled

ROSINWEED
Silphium integrifolium Michx.

ROSINWEED
Silphium integrifolium Michx.

Perennial herbs with the Greek name for another plant also producing resin.

Family Asteraceae, or Aster Family

Flowers The yellow heads are up to 5 cm wide. They are composed of both disk and ray flowers. The rays are about 0.5 cm long and number up to 25.

Leaves Opposite, ovate-lanceolate, acuminate, entire or toothed, and rough to the touch. They are sessile, from 7 to 15 cm long, and 2.5 to 5 cm wide.

Use or Importance Rosinweed is palatable and nutritious when young and is readily grazed. It decreases when the prairie is grazed.

Habitat Common in Illinois prairies.

Distribution in Illinois

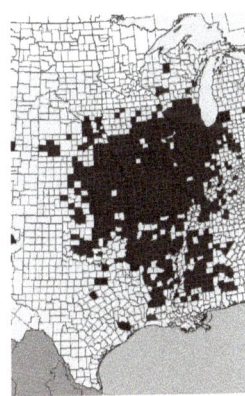

Distribution in central USA

Group C. Leaves simple, opposite or whorled

CUP-PLANT
Silphium perfoliatum L.

CUP-PLANT
Silphium perfoliatum L.

Perennial herbs with the Greek name for another plant also producing resin.

Family Asteraceae, or Aster Family

Flowers The heads are numerous and composed of both disk and ray flowers. These heads are 2.5 to 7.5 cm wide, yellow, with 20 to 30 rays. Each ray is about 2.5 cm long.

Leaves The leaves are a distinguishing part of the plant, being broadly triangular to ovate. The upper leaves are connate-perfoliate, or clasping on the squarrish, stout stems, forming a cup-like junction. The lower leaves have blades which contract into winged petioles. The larger leaves are up to 35 cm long and to 20 cm wide.

Use or Importance Cup-plant is palatable, and decreases under grazing.

Habitat Prairies, open woods, and other mostly open areas.

Distribution in Illinois
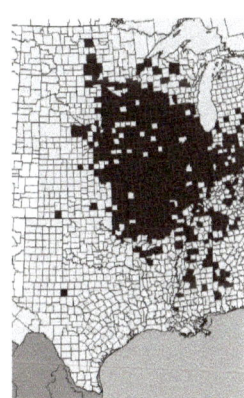
Distribution in central USA

Group C. Leaves simple, opposite or whorled

AMERICAN GERMANDER
Teucrium canadense L.

AMERICAN GERMANDER

Teucrium canadense L.

The Greek name, probably named for Teucer, first king of Troy, who first used the plant in medicine.

Family Lamiaceae, or Mint Family

Season and Stature American Germander, also known as Wood Sage, is a native, warm-season perennial attaining a height up to 60 cm. It flowers from June to the end of Summer.

Flowers The spikes are dense and up to 25 cm long. The two-lipped flowers are about 1 cm long, on very short pedicels. The flowers are tubular and pinkish in color.

Leaves The arrangement of leaves on the square stems is opposite. The leaves are prominently pinnately veined, oblong-lanceolate to ovate-lanceolate, pointed at the tip, and rounded at the base. The margins are toothed, and the leaves are hairy beneath.

Use or Importance This species has little importance as a forage plant.

Habitat Moist prairies, and at the edge of thickets.

 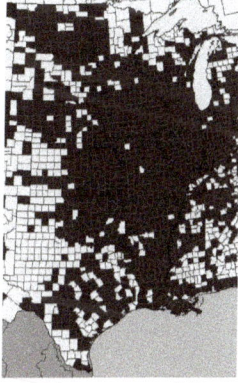

Distribution in Illinois   *Distribution in central USA*

CULVER'S-ROOT
Veronicastrum virginicum (L.) Farw.

CULVER'S-ROOT

Veronicastrum virginicum (L.) Farw.   Resembles *Veronica,* genus name in honor of Saint Veronica.

Family Plantaginaceae, or Plantain Family

Season and Stature Culver's-root is a native, warm-season, perennial herb, which attains a height of up to 1.5 meters. It flowers from June to September.

Flowers The flowers are borne in several spike-like racemes. The racemes are 6 to 20 cm long. Flowers are densely crowded on the racemes; the corollas are tubular, white to pale bluish in color and about 2 mm long.

Leaves The leaves are verticillate or whorled in 3 to several leaves at each node (opposite in some of the uppermost leaves). The leaf is about 7 to 20 cm long, and 2.5 cm wide, serrulate, and narrowed at the base.

Use or Importance Culver's-root is also known as Culver's physic. Apparently the root has cathartic qualities.

Habitat In Illinois, often along railroad and highway rights-of-way where relict patches of prairie occur. Typical habitat is one with good soil and moist conditions; however, it also occurs in dry woods.

Distribution in Illinois

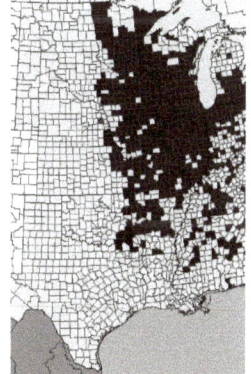

Distribution in central USA

Group C. Leaves simple, opposite or whorled

GROUP D

Leaves simple, alternate.

PUSSY-TOES (*Antennaria neglecta*), p. 145
PRAIRIE SAGE (*Artemisia ludoviciana*), p. 147
INDIAN PLANTAIN (*Arnoglossum plantagineum*), p. 149
HAIRY GREEN MILKWEED (*Asclepias hirtella*), p. 151
BUTTERFLY WEED (*Asclepias tuberosa*), p. 153
GREEN MILKWEED (*Asclepias viridiflora*), p. 155
FALSE BONESET (*Brickellia eupatorioides*), p. 157
CLUSTERED POPPY MALLOW (*Callirhoe triangulata*), p. 159
NEW JERSEY TEA (*Ceanothus americana*), p. 161
FALSE TOADFLAX (*Comandra umbellata*), p. 163
PALE PRAIRIE CONEFLOWER (*Echinacea pallida*), p. 165
FLAT-TOPPED SPURGE (*Euphorbia corollata*), p. 167
GRASS-LLEAVED GOLDENROD (*Euthamnia graminifolia*), p. 169
SAWTOOTH SUNFLOWER (*Helianthus grosseserratus*), p. 171
JERUSALEM ARTICHOKE (*Helianthus tuberosus*), p. 173
ROUGH BLAZING-STAR (*Liatris aspera*), p. 175
TALL GAYFEATHER (*Liatris pycnostachya*), p. 177

GROUP D

Leaves simple, alternate.

SCALY BLAZING-STAR (*Liatris squarrosa*), p. 179
HOARY PUCCOON (*Lithospermum canescens*), p. 181
SPIKED LOBELIA (*Lobelia spicata*), p. 183
COMMON SUNDROPS (*Oenothera pilosella*), p. 185
PRAIRIE GROUNDSEL (*Packera paupercula*), p. 187
AMERICAN FEVERFEW (*Parthenium intergrifolium*), p. 189
BROWN-EYED SUSAN (*Rudbeckia hirta*), p. 191
PRAIRIE WILLOW (*Salix humilis*), p. 193
COMPASS PLANT (*Silphium laciniatum*), p. 195
TALL GOLDENROD (*Solidago canadensis*), p. 197
STIFF GOLDENROD (*Solidago rigida*), p. 199
HEATH ASTER (*Symphyotrichum ericoides*), p. 201
SMOOTH ASTER (*Symphyotrichum laeve*), p. 203
NEW ENGLAND ASTER (*Symphyotrichum novae-angliae*), p. 205
AROMATIC ASTER (*Symphyotrichum oblongifolium*), p. 207
SKY-BLUE ASTER (*Symphyotrichum oolentangiense*), p. 209
SILKY ASTER (*Symphyotrichum sericeum*), p. 211

PUSSY-TOES
Antennaria neglecta Greene

PUSSY-TOES

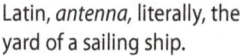

Antennaria neglecta Greene

Latin, *antenna*, literally, the yard of a sailing ship.

Family Asteraceae, or Aster Family

Season and Stature This Pussy-toes is a small native perennial reaching a height of 40 cm. It blooms during the Spring and Summer.

Flowers Each white flowering head is composed only of disk flowers. Several heads are grouped together at the top of a slender, sparsely leafy stem.

Leaves Most leaves are in a basal rosette; these leaves are broader than the leaves found on the stem. Leaves are covered on the lower surface by a cobwebby mass of white hairs.

Use or Importance The flowers, which are long-persistent, have been used in winter bouquets.

Habitat: Dry prairies and woods.

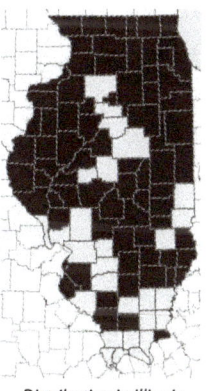

Distribution in Illinois

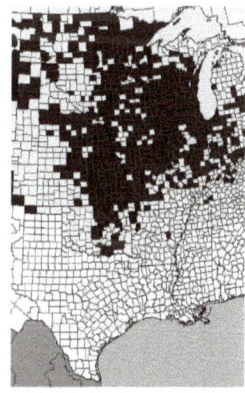

Distribution in central USA

Group D. Leaves simple, alternate.

INDIAN PLANTAIN
Arnoglossum plantagineum Raf.

INDIAN PLANTAIN
Arnoglossum plantagineum Raf.

Synonym *Cacalia tuberosa* Nutt.

Family Asteraceae, or Aster Family

Season and Stature Indian Plantain is a native, warm-season perennial. It grows to 1-2 meters tall, and blooms during the Summer.

Flowers The heads are very numerous in a compound inflorescence. Each head is about 3 mm wide and cream-colored.

Leaves Basal leaves oval, ovate, or ovate-lanceolate, usually entire, narrowed at the base, petioled, and 5- to 9-veined. Upper leaves are ovate to oblong and sessile or on short petioles. The upper leaves are often toothed toward their tip.

Use or Importance Indian Plantain has a fleshy tuber which is reportedly edible.

Habitat Wet prairies, moist fields.

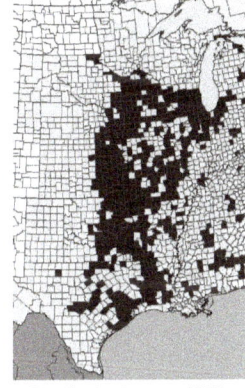

Distribution in Illinois *Distribution in central USA*

PRAIRIE SAGE
Artemisia ludoviciana Nutt.

PRAIRIE SAGE
Artemisia ludoviciana Nutt.

Named in honor of Artemis, the Greek goddess of chastity.

Family Asteraceae, or Aster Family

Season and Stature Prairie Sage, also called Western Sage, White Sage, or Mugwort, is a native, warm-season perennial. It grows to a height of 30 to 100 cm.

Flowers The small flowers are borne in spike-like panicles, and are whitish-green.

Leaves The leaves are the striking part of the plant. They are covered with a white tomentum on both sides, giving the whole plant a light gray-green color. The leaves are lanceolate, oblong, 2.5 to 8 cm long, and over 0.5 cm wide. The leaves may be entire, or the lower ones may be toothed or lobed. The leaves are narrowed into short petioles.

Use or Importance Prairie Sage is frequent in garden plantings. It is often used as a border because of its silvery-white foliage contrast.

Habitat Sandy places, as along highways and railroads; becoming more common in the arid West.

 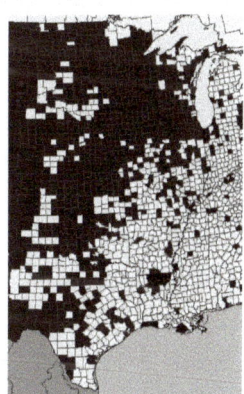

Distribution in Illinois   *Distribution in central USA*

Group D. Leaves simple, alternate.

HAIRY GREEN MILKWEED
Asclepias hirtella (Pennell) Woods.

D

HAIRY GREEN MILKWEED

Asclepias hirtella (Pennell) Woods.   The Greek name for these plants, in honor of Asclepias, god of medicine.

Family Asclepiadaceae, or Milkweed Family

Season and Stature Hairy Green Milkweed is a native, warm-season perennial which may grow to a height of one meter. It flowers during the Summer.

Flowers Hairy Green Milkweed has the typical hour-glass shaped flowers of milkweeds. Several greenish flowers are borne in groups from the axils of the leaves.

Leaves The alternate or opposite leaves are linear to linear-lanceolate and rough to the touch. There is latex present.

Use or Importance This milkweed is known for producing many flowers. It is attractive to butterflies and bees, mostly notably honeybees, bumble-bees, and leaf-cutting bees.

Habitat Dry prairies.

Distribution in Illinois

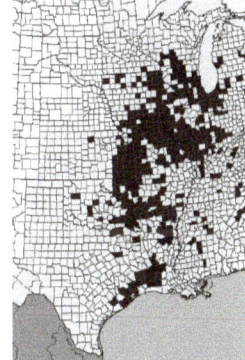

Distribution in central USA

Group D. Leaves simple, alternate.

BUTTERFLY WEED
Asclepias tuberosa L.

BUTTERFLY WEED

Asclepias tuberosa L.

The Greek name for these plants, in honor of Asclepias, god of medicine.

Family Asclepiadaceae, or Milkweed Family

Season and Stature Butterfly Weed is a native, warm-season perennial which grows to a height up to 70 cm. It flowers in the Summer and into the Fall.

Flowers The orange-colored flowers are borne in a broad umbel and, like all milkweed flowers, are pinched at the middle with 5 downward flexed petals and a corona at the top to give the flowers somewhat of an hourglass shape.

Leaves Unlike most milkweeds, Butterfly Weed has alternate leaves and, when plucked, the leaves do not exude a white latex as other milkweeds do. The sap of this milkweed is cream-colored and thin-looking in contrast to the sap of most other milkweeds. The leaves are tapered at each end and are without distinct petioles.

Use or Importance This species can be propagated readily from seed, and has been used as an ornamental plant (and is especially attractive to butterflies). It is reported that in its young stages it can be boiled as greens and that Indians used its roots as medicine. Livestock will not eat it by choice; it behaves as an increaser or invader on range land.

Habitat Dry, open places. It is a common plant of the prairie flora.

Distribution in Illinois　　Distribution in central USA

Group D. Leaves simple, alternate.

GREEN MILKWEED
Asclepias viridiflora Raf.

GREEN MILKWEED

Asclepias viridiflora Raf. The Greek name for these plants, in honor of Asclepias, god of medicine.

Synonym *Acerates viridiflora* (Raf.) Pursh ex Eat.

Family Asclepiadaceae, or Milkweed Family

Season and Stature Green Milkweed is a native, warm-season, perennial herb growing to 30 to 90 cm tall. It flowers from June to September.

Flowers The flowers are borne in dense terminal and axillary umbels. Pedicels are 4 to 8 mm long. The flowers are green and have an hour-glass shape. This shape is typical for milkweed flowers and is due to a structure on the flower known as a corona.

Leaves Slightly rough to touch, alternate or opposite, oval, oblong, or ovate to lanceolate. The leaves are 2.5 to 12 cm long and to 4 cm wide. They have short petioles.

Use or Importance The flowers attract bumblebees and other long-tongued bees, which are the most common pollinators.

Habitat In Illinois, found in dry upland prairies, hill prairies, and sand prairies.

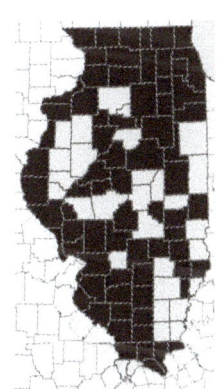
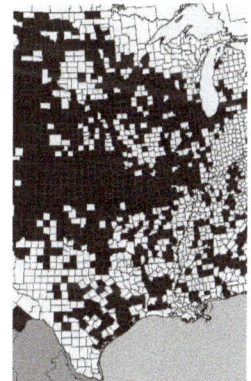

Distribution in Illinois *Distribution in central USA*

Group D. Leaves simple, alternate.

FALSE BONESET
Brickellia eupatorioides (L.) Shinners

FALSE BONESET

Brickellia eupatorioides (L.) Shinners

Synonym *Kuhnia eupatorioides* L.

Family Asteraceae, or Aster Family

Herbs or small shrubs named in honor of Dr. John Brickell, 18th-century American naturalist, who published *A Natural History of North Carolina* (1737).

Season and Stature False Boneset is a native, warm-season perennial. It attains a height of nearly one meter, and blooms during the Fall. Its roots have been reported to extend downward in the soil for more than 5 meters.

Flowers The heads are numerous, peduncled, and loosely clustered in a terminal inflorescence with a somewhat flattened look. The flowers are whitish. The heads are all discoid, with no rays present.

Leaves The leaves are alternately arranged on the stems. The leaves are linear-lanceolate, acute at the apex, narrowed to the base, short-petioled or sessile, and sparingly toothed.

Use or Importance Little use has been attributed to this plant.

Habitat Dry woods and prairies.

Distribution in Illinois

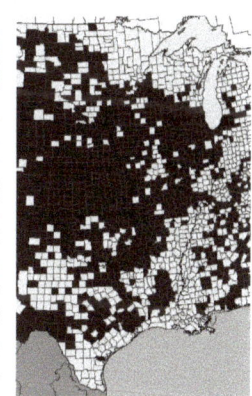
Distribution in central USA

Group D. Leaves simple, alternate.

CLUSTERED POPPY MALLOW
Callirhoe triangulata (Leavenworth) Gray

CLUSTERED POPPY MALLOW

Callirhoe triangulata (Leavenworth) Gray

Showy herbs named in honor of the daughter of a minor Greek deity, Achelous, a river god.

Family Malvaceae, or Mallow Family

Season and Stature Clustered Poppy Mallow is a native, warm-season perennial. It attains a height of 35 to 70 cm. It blooms during the Summer, from June to August.

Flowers The flowers are borne in terminal panicled clusters. Each flower is deep purple, and 2.5 to 5.0 cm wide.

Leaves The leaves are triangular-hastate or spear-shaped. The lower leaves have long petioles, while the upper leaves are short-petioled or nearly sessile.

Use or Importance This handsome herb is a decreaser under grazing and disappears when grazing is uncontrolled.

Habitat Sandy habitats.

Distribution in Illinois

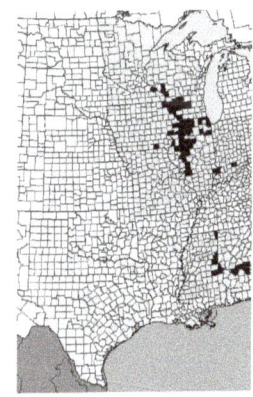
Distribution in central USA

Group D. Leaves simple, alternate.

NEW JERSEY TEA
Ceanothus americanus L.

NEW JERSEY TEA

Ceanothus americanus L.

From the Greek name for a spiny plant (not this one).

Family Rhamnaceae, or Buckthorn Family

Season and Stature New Jersey Tea is a native, cool-season shrub. It attains a height of about one meter. New Jersey Tea flowers during late Spring.

Flowers The flowers are borne in terminal or axillary corymbs or panicles. The white flowers are on pedicels less than 1 cm long.

Leaves Alternate, ovate to oblong, up to 6 cm long, and to 3 cm wide. They are usually hairy on the lower surface.

Use or Importance The leaves of this species may be used to brew a tea. The plant is grazed when young and tends to disappear when prairies are overgrazed.

Habitat Dry open woods, rocky slopes, prairie borders.

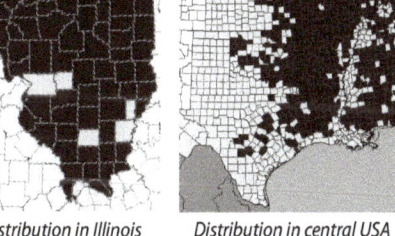

Distribution in Illinois   *Distribution in central USA*

FALSE TOADFLAX

D

Comandra umbellata (L.) Nutt.

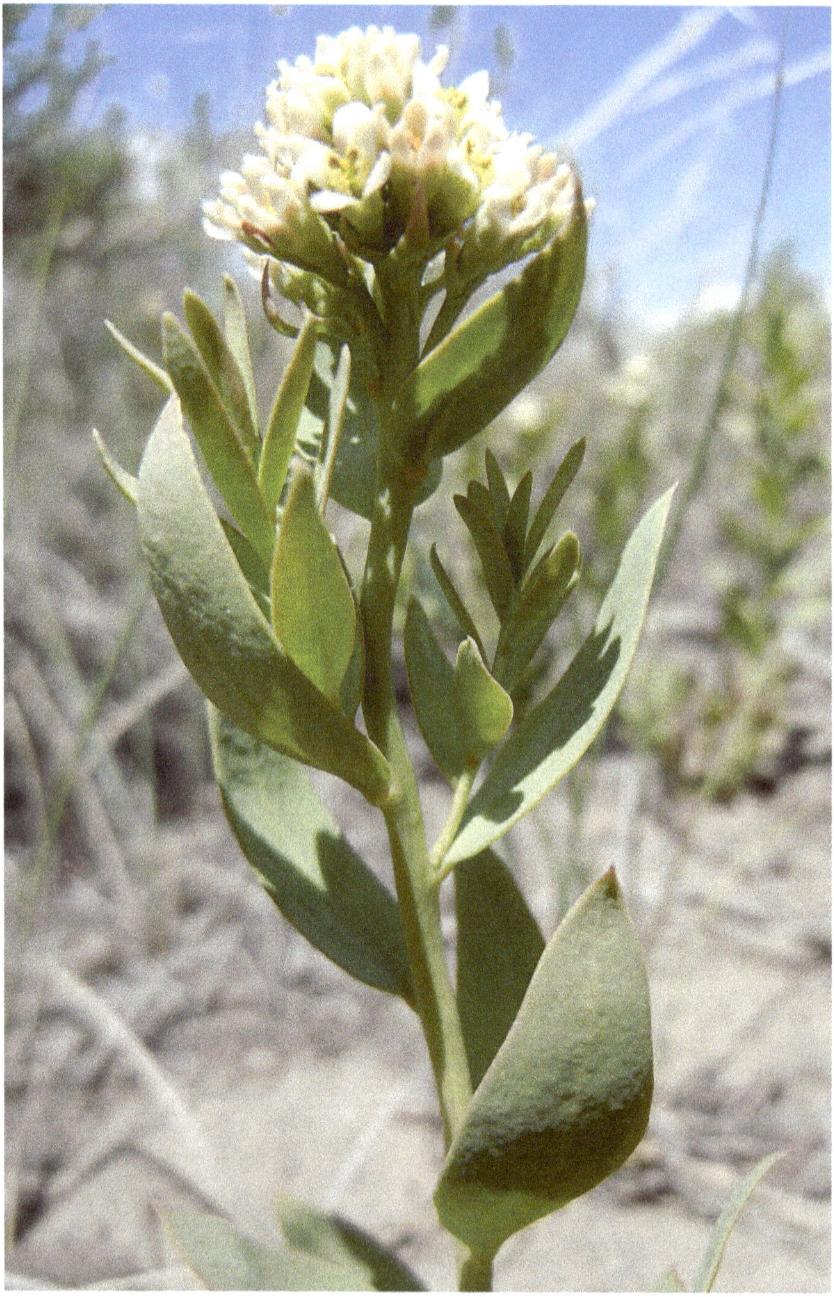

FALSE TOADFLAX

Comandra umbellata (L.) Nutt.

From the Greek words *kome* (hair) and *andros* (male, stamen); in reference to the bearded stamens.

Synonym *Comandra richardsiana* Fern.

Family Santalaceae, or Sandalwood Family

Season and Stature False Toadflax is a small, warm-season, native herb. It attains a height of 10 to 15 cm, and blooms from May to August.

Flowers Creamy white, with 4 stamens which are opposite the perianth lobes. There are no petals, but the sepals are whitish and petal-like. The cymes are several-flowered, becoming corymbose at the summit of the plant. The flowers are axillary, with short pedicels.

Leaves The leaves are numerous, ascending, alternate on the stem, oblong or oblong-lanceolate, acute at each end, and sessile.

Use or Importance This small plant lives as a partial parasite on the roots of various trees.

Habitat In Illinois, occurs as an occasional species of dry prairies and open woods.

Distribution in Illinois

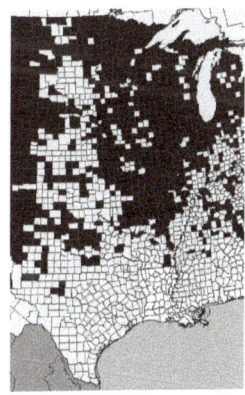

Distribution in central USA

PALE PRAIRIE CONEFLOWER
Echinacea pallida (Nutt.) Nutt.

PALE PRAIRIE CONEFLOWER

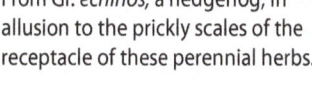

Echinacea pallida (Nutt.) Nutt.

From Gr. *echinos,* a hedgehog; in allusion to the prickly scales of the receptacle of these perennial herbs.

Family Asteraceae, or Aster Family

Season and Stature Pale Prairie Coneflower is one of the handsomest of our prairie wildflowers. It is a warm-season perennial, growing to 60 cm.

Flowers Each head is about 4 cm wide (the central disk is about 2.5 cm wide). The rays are pinkish and extend slightly downward. After the rays drop off, the seed head turns a dark brown color.

Leaves The plant produces a few ovate-lanceolate leaves at ground level. These basal leaves are up to 20 cm long and 3 to 4 cm broad. The leaves are harshly pubescent and have about 3 prominent veins. Smaller leaves extend up the stems.

Use or Importance Besides its natural beauty and adaptability as a garden plant, this species is grazed and contributes toward roughage in livestock diets. It decreases under grazing.

Habitat Prairies.

Distribution in Illinois

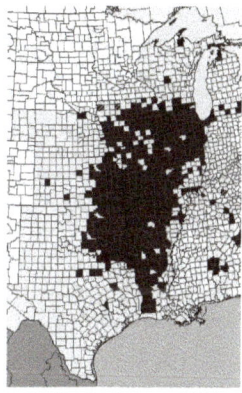

Distribution in central USA

Group D. Leaves simple, alternate.

FLAT-TOPPED SPURGE
Euphorbia corollata L.

FLAT-TOPPED SPURGE

Euphorbia corollata L.

Classically supposed to have been named for one Euphorbus, physician to the king of Mauretania.

Family Euphorbiaceae, or Spurge Family

Season and Stature Flat-topped Spurge is a native, warm-season perennial herb. It attains a height of about one meter. This species blooms during the Summer.

Flowers Several white flowers are arranged in a cymosely branched inflorescence which spreads to a width of 15 to 20 cm. The flowers are without petals, but there are five white petal-like appendages. The ovary is 3-lobed.

Leaves Linear-oblong, 1 to 2 cm long, entire, short-petioled or sessile. The leaves at the base of the inflorescence are several in a whorl. The entire plant contains milky sap.

Use or Importance Flat-topped Spurge is one of the top ranking upland herbs of the True Prairie in abundance. However, it tends to disappear from prairies which are too heavily grazed.

Habitat Common in prairies, dry woods, fields, and roadsides.

Distribution in Illinois   Distribution in central USA

Group D. Leaves simple, alternate.

GRASS-LEAVED GOLDENROD
Euthamnia graminifolia (L.) Nutt.

GRASS-LEAVED GOLDENROD
Euthamnia graminifolia (L.) Nutt.

Synonym *Solidago graminifolia* (L.) Salisb.

Family Asteraceae, or Aster Family

Season and Stature The Grass-leaved Goldenrod is a native, warm-season perennial. It reaches a height up to 120 cm, and blooms during the Summer.

Flowers The yellow ray flowers are pistillate and more numerous than the disk flowers, which are perfect. The rays number from 12 to 20, the disk flowers from 8 to 12. The heads are in somewhat flat-topped inflorescences.

Leaves The leaves are linear-lanceolate, numerous, narrowed at each end, up to 15 cm long and to 0.5 cm wide; they have 3 to 5 veins.

Use or Importance Virtually all species of Goldenrod take easily to cultivation. Most species possess aromatic, mildly stimulating properties used for teas. They are very attractive in the autumn landscape.

Habitat Prairies and fields.

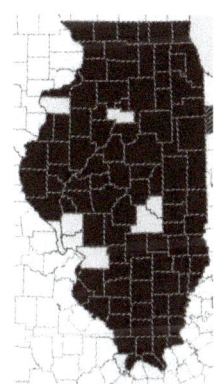

Distribution in Illinois

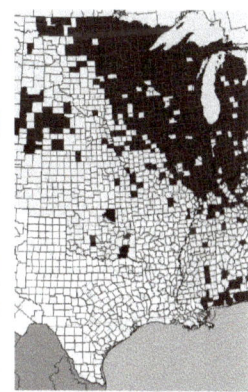

Distribution in central USA

Group D. Leaves simple, alternate.

SAWTOOTH SUNFLOWER
Helianthus grosseserratus Martens

SAWTOOTH SUNFLOWER

Helianthus grosseserratus Martens

From Gr. *helios,* the sun; *anthos,* a flower.

Season and Stature Sawtooth Sunflower is a native, warm-season perennial herb. It attains a height of up to 2.5 meters, and flowers during the Fall.

Flowers The ray flowers are neutral; the disk flowers are perfect and fertile. The heads are numerous, 3 to 7 cm wide, with 10 to 20 deep yellow rays. The disk is yellowish.

Leaves The leaves are long-lanceolate, with slender petioles. The upper leaves are alternate, the lower ones opposite. Leaves are sharply serrate, rough above, hairy beneath, 10 to 20 cm long, and up to 2.5 cm wide.

Use or Importance The presence of this species was formerly used to indicate high quality land for growing corn.

Habitat In Illinois, occurs in all parts of the state, and in every moist or lowland prairie type.

Distribution in Illinois

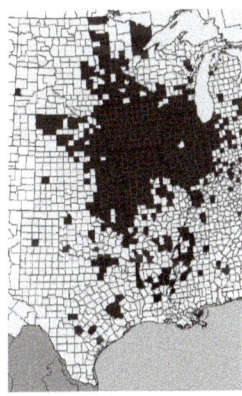

Distribution in central USA

JERUSALEM ARTICHOKE
Helianthus tuberosus L.

JERUSALEM ARTICHOKE
Helianthus tuberosus L.

From Gr. *helios*, the sun; *anthos*, a flower.

Family Asteraceae, or Aster Family

Season and Stature Jerusalem Artichoke is a native, warm-season perennial. The plant is large, reaching a height of up to 3 meters. It blooms during the late-Summer and Fall.

Flowers There are several yellow heads on each plant, each measuring up to 8 cm wide. The rays, number from 12 to 20, and both the rays and the disk are yellow.

Leaves Ovate, ovate-oblong, or ovate-lanceolate, 3-veined, narrowed at the base, petiolate, rough to the touch, and serrate. They are up to 20 cm long and to 7 cm wide. The upper leaves are alternate, while the lower ones are generally opposite.

Use or Importance Jerusalem Artichoke has thickened, starchy tubers which are edible. The plant is adaptable to cultivation and the tubers are available commercially, sometimes under the brand-name "Sunchoke."

Habitat This species grows in wet prairies, damp woods, and along roads.

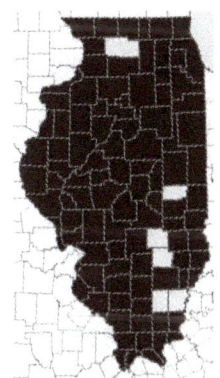
Distribution in Illinois

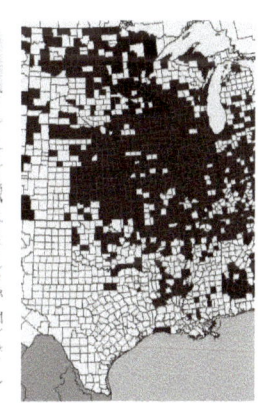
Distribution in central USA

Group D. Leaves simple, alternate.

ROUGH BLAZING-STAR
Liatris aspera Michx.

ROUGH BLAZING-STAR

Liatris aspera Michx.

Family Asteraceae, or Aster Family

Season and Stature Rough Blazing-star is a native, warm-season perennial herb. It grows to about 90 cm tall, and blooms during the Fall.

Flowers The inflorescence is an elongated spike, to nearly 60 cm long. The heads on the spike number from 20, to over 100 or more; each is about 25- to 40-flowered, and purple in color. The heads are about 1.5 to 2.5 cm broad.

Leaves Upper leaves are linear, scabrous, and slightly ciliate. The lower leaves are 1 to 2 cm wide. The leaves are alternate and are borne along the entire length of the stem, decreasing somewhat in size toward the summit.

Use or Importance In the past, Rough Blazing-Star was thought to be good for treating rattlesnake bites. The corms were used for this unproved treatment. Mainly, these plants are important aesthetically as they brighten the yellows of autumn with contrasting purple.

Habitat Dry or sandy soil; in Illinois, present on several types of prairie.

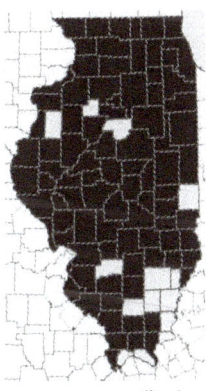
Distribution in Illinois
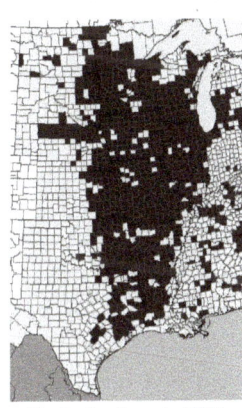
Distribution in central USA

Group D. Leaves simple, alternate.

TALL GAYFEATHER
Liatris pycnostachya Michx.

TALL GAYFEATHER
Liatris pycnostachya Michx.

Family Asteraceae, or Aster Family

Season and Stature Tall Gayfeather is a native, warm-season perennial. It is a long lived plant with roots penetrating to over fifteen feet. It attains a height of 1.5 meters.

Flowers The flowers are borne close to the upper end of the stem in dense clusters. The rose-purple flowers are very showy.

Leaves Short hairs exist on both the stems and leaves so that the entire plant has a stiff, harsh look. The leaves are narrow or linear, and are longest at the lower end of the plant and are progressively shorter near the flowers.

Use or Importance Tall Gayfeather is grazed by livestock and is classed as a decreaser by range managers. The plant is often associated with Big Bluestem, and is conspicuous from a distance. When the blossoms are collected and dried, they preserve well as an indoor decoration.

Habitat Lowland prairies.

Distribution in Illinois
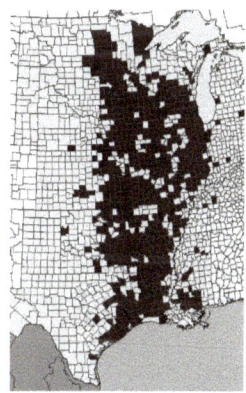
Distribution in central USA

Group D. Leaves simple, alternate.

SCALY BLAZING STAR
Liatris squarrosa (L.) Michx.

SCALY BLAZING-STAR
Liatris squarrosa (L.) Michx.

Family Asteraceae, or Aster Family

Season and Stature Scaly Blazing-Star, also known as 'Colic Root', is a native, warm-season perennial herb. It attains a height of 15 to 60 cm, and blooms during the Fall.

Flowers The heads are sessile or on short peduncles and bear from 15 to 60 flowers. The heads, which are up to 3 cm high and about half as wide, are rose-purple. The bracts at the base of each head are in 5 to 7 series, lanceolate, acuminate, and spreading.

Leaves Narrowly linear, stiff, dotted, up to 15 cm long, and 3 to 4 mm wide. They are alternate along the stem.

Use or Importance Scaly Blazing-Star decreases under heavy grazing.

Habitat Dry woods and prairies.

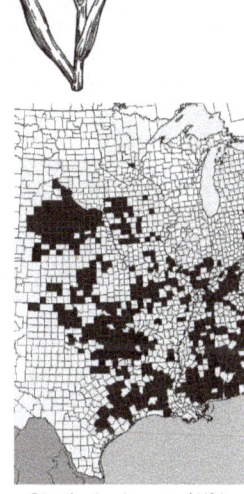

Distribution in Illinois

Distribution in central USA

HOARY PUCCOON
Lithospermum canescens (Michx.) Lehm.

HOARY PUCCOON

Lithospermum canescens (Michx.) Lehm.   The classical name.

Family Boraginaceae, or Borage Family

Season and Stature Hoary Puccoon is a native, cool-season perennial. It attains a height of 15 to 45 cm and flowers from April to June.

Flowers The flowers are orange-yellow. The corolla is tubular and composed of five lobes which are rounded at their tips. The flowers are less than 1 cm long and are borne in dense, short, leafy racemes.

Leaves The sessile leaves, which are hairy when young, are oblong-linear, tapering to each end.

Use or Importance The presence of Hoary Puccoon is an indicator of prairie in good condition. The plant decreases when grazed.

Habitat Dry prairies, dry woods.

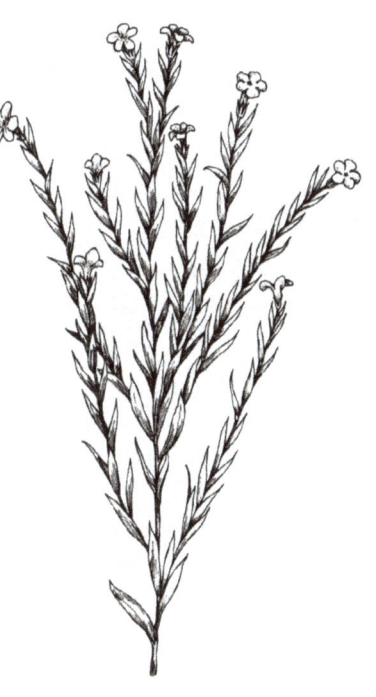

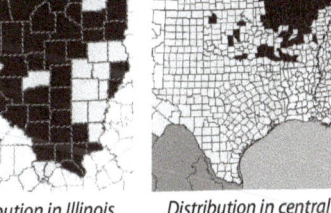

Distribution in Illinois   *Distribution in central USA*

SPIKED LOBELIA
Lobelia spicata Lam.

SPIKED LOBELIA

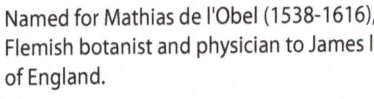

Lobelia spicata Lam.

Named for Mathias de l'Obel (1538-1616), Flemish botanist and physician to James I of England.

Family Campanulaceae, or Bellflower Family

Season and Stature The Spiked Lobelia is a native, warm-season perennial to about one meter tall. It flowers during the Summer. Spiked Lobelia was formerly placed in the Lobeliaceae, or Lobelia Family.

Flowers The pale blue flowers are about 0.5 cm long, dense to distant on spicate racemes which are over 30 cm long. The flower is 5-parted, irregular and tubular. There are 2 short petals and 3 larger ones.

Leaves The leaves are toothed or entire. The basal leaves are broadly oblong, oval, or obovate, narrowed into short petioles and up to 7 cm long. The upper leaves are sessile, spatulate, and smaller.

Use or Importance The leaves of many lobelias are acrid and contain poisonous substances. A number of drugs and medicines were formerly obtained from them.

Habitat Woods, prairies, and fields.

Distribution in Illinois

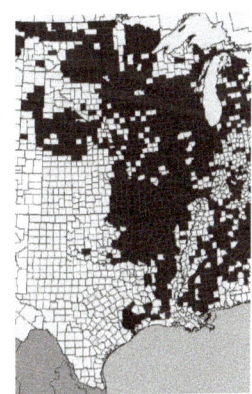

Distribution in central USA

Group D. Leaves simple, alternate.

COMMON SUNDROPS

D

Oenothera pilosella Raf.

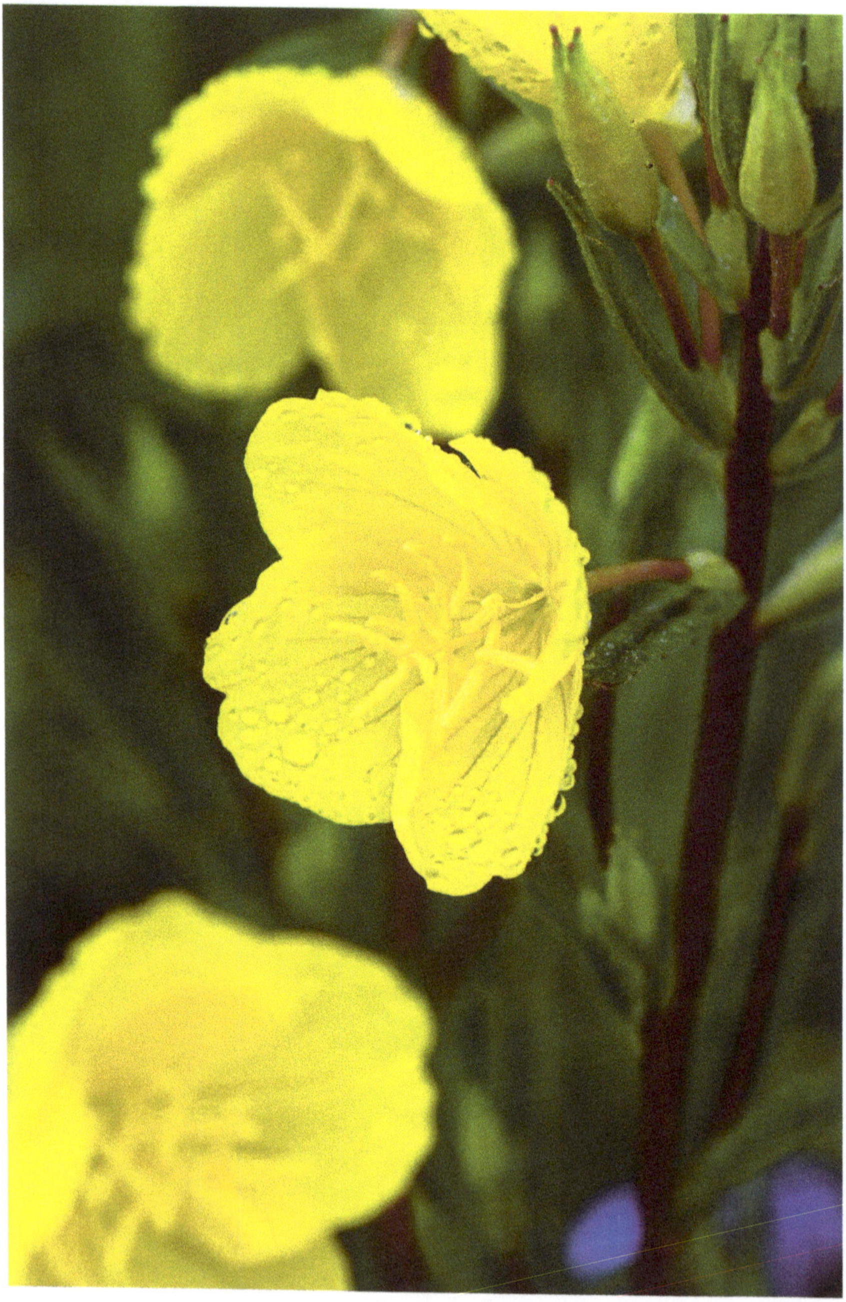

COMMON SUNDROPS

Oenothera pilosella Raf.

The Greek name, which is supposed to derive from *oinos*, wine; *thera*, booty.

Family Onagraceae, or Evening-Primrose Family

Season and Stature Common Sundrops is a native warm-season perennial. It reaches a height of up to 90 cm, and blooms during the Summer.

Flowers The flowers are bright yellow and open in the morning and the evening. Flowers are 2.5 to 5 cm wide, and borne in terminal, leafy-bracted spikes.

Leaves The leaf shape is lanceolate, ovate, or oval-lanceolate; acute or somewhat obtuse at the tip; narrowed and sessile at the base; and with the lower leaves petioled. The leaves margins and stems coarsely hairy.

Use or Importance Owing to the brilliance and beauty of this species, it is sometimes planted in gardens.

Habitat Mostly in dry soil in upland situations; may be expected in all prairie types except the wettest.

Distribution in Illinois

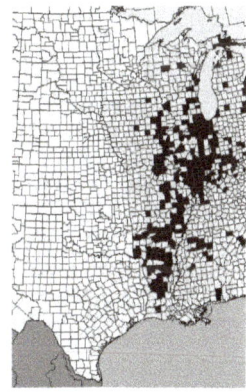

Distribution in central USA

Group D. Leaves simple, alternate.

PRAIRIE GROUNDSEL
Packera paupercula (Michx.) A.&D. Löve

PRAIRIE GROUNDSEL

Packera paupercula (Michx.) A.&D. Löve

Senecio, Latin, *senex,* an old man; from the hoary pappus of these herbs.

Synonym *Senecio pauperculus* Michx.

Family Asteraceae, or Aster Family

Season and Stature Prairie Groundsel is a warm-season perennial. It reaches a height of 50 cm, and blooms during the late Spring and early Summer.

Flowers There are several yellow flower heads at the top of the stem. Each head is up to 2 cm across and has several yellow rays.

Leaves Several more or less elliptic, long-petiolate leaves are clustered at the base of the plant. The leaves on the stem are alternate and usually deeply incised.

Use or Importance Prairie Groundsel adds brightness to the prairie scene during the late Spring.

Habitat Prairies, cliffs.

Distribution in Illinois

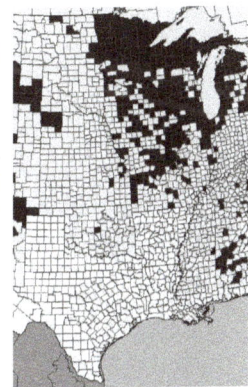

Distribution in central USA

Group D. Leaves simple, alternate.

AMERICAN FEVERFEW
Parthenium integrifolium L.

AMERICAN FEVERFEW

Parthenium integrifolium L.   Greek name for some plant with white ray flowers.

Family Asteraceae, or Aster Family

Season and Stature American Feverfew is a native, warm-season perennial, having tuberous thickened rootstocks. The plant attains a height of up to one meter. It begins flowering during the Summer and extends into September.

Flowers The heads are numerous in dense terminal clusters. The disk flowers are perfect but not fertile. The whitish ray flowers are about 5 in number, pistillate and fertile.

Leaves American Feverfew has firm, rough leaves which are ovate or ovate-oblong with margins which are crenate-dentate. The lower stem leaves and basal leaves are petioled. The leaves are up to 30 cm long and to 10 cm or more wide.

Use or Importance A tea from the leaves has historically been used in treating fever. The plant is also called wild quinine.

Habitat Dry prairies, roadsides, and along railroads.

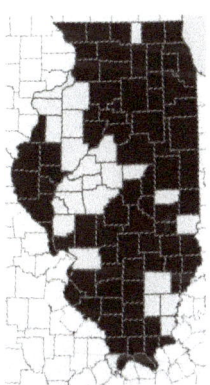
Distribution in Illinois

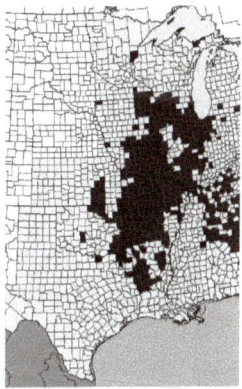
Distribution in central USA

BROWN-EYED SUSAN
Rudbeckia hirta L.

BROWN-EYED SUSAN

Rudbeckia hirta L.

Named for Olaf Rudbeck (1660-1740), Professor of Botany at Uppsala and a teacher of Linnaeus.

Family Asteraceae, or Aster Family

Season and Stature The handsome, familiar, Brown-eyed Susan is a native, warm-season perennial herb. Brown-eyed Susan grows to a height of 70 cm. It flowers throughout the late-Summer and into the Fall.

Flowers The showy yellow rays, 10 to 20 in number, are about 1.5 to 2 cm long. The brown disk is about 1.5 to 2 cm wide and dome-shaped. Each head is about 6-7 cm wide.

Leaves The lower leaves are oblong, toothed, and somewhat hairy or rough. The upper leaves are oblong-lanceolate, smaller, sessile, and alternate in their arrangement on the hairy stems.

Use or Importance This plant is often grown in gardens because of its showy flowers. It is not a palatable species for grazing.

Habitat This species is found in all Illinois prairies. In some southwestern Illinois hill prairies, a shorter, later-blooming species is present: *Rudbeckia missouriensis*.

Distribution in Illinois

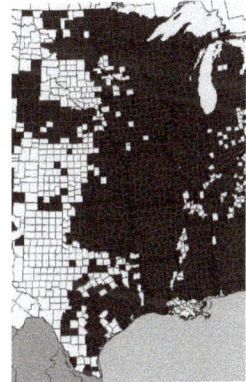
Distribution in central USA

PRAIRIE WILLOW
Salix humilis Marsh.

PRAIRIE WILLOW

Salix humilis Marsh.
The Latin name.

Family Salicaceae, or Willow Family

Season and Stature Prairie Willow is a low shrub. It grows to 2 meters high, but less than this when repeatedly mowed. Prairie Willow is a cool-season plant which blooms during April and May.

Flowers The flowering spikes, or catkins, appear much before the leaves, and contain either male or female flowers. Plants are dioecious, that is, the male and female flowers are borne on separate plants. The catkins are sessile, oblong-ovoid, and dense. The female, or pistillate, catkins are about 2.5 to 3.0 cm long in fruit.

Leaves Oblanceolate, petioled, up to 15 cm long, and to one cm wide. They taper to each end. The upper surface is dark green, the lower is densely gray-hairy. The leaves have obliquely lanceolate to ovate stipules.

Use or Importance Twigs of all willows are very pliable, which makes them useful in basketry. The Prairie Willow can be used in this manner.

Habitat Dry soil of prairies.

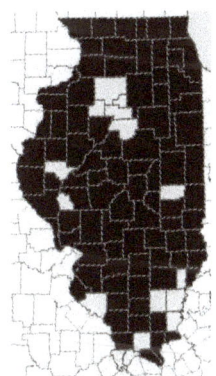
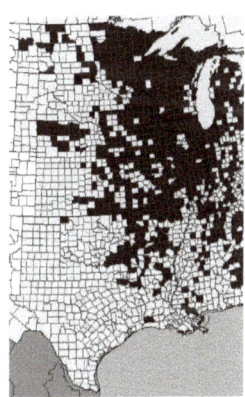

Distribution in Illinois   *Distribution in central USA*

Group D. Leaves simple, alternate.

COMPASS PLANT
Silphium laciniatum L.

COMPASS PLANT

Silphium laciniatum L.

Perennial herbs with the Greek name for another plant also producing resin.

Family Asteraceae, or Aster Family

Flowers The yellow heads are borne at the tips of the branches. Each head has both ray and disk flowers. The green bracts on the back of each head are in more than 2 series.

Leaves Large, deeply cleft, and rough to the touch. They are usually placed edgewise in a north-south direction, hence the common name.

Use or Importance Compass Plant was important in the diet of bison, and it is eaten by cattle. The plant is a decreaser when grazed.

Habitat A common prairie inhabitant.

Distribution in Illinois

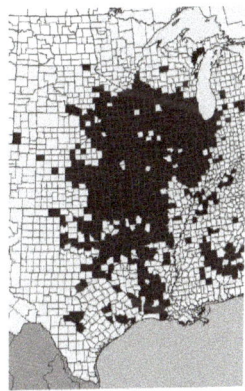

Distribution in central USA

Group D. Leaves simple, alternate.

TALL GOLDENROD
Solidago canadensis L.

TALL GOLDENROD
Solidago canadensis L.

Latin, *solido*, to make whole; in allusion to the reputed healing qualities of these perennial herbs.

Family Asteraceae, or Aster Family

Flowers The yellow heads are borne in abundance on spreading or recurving branches of the large panicle. The individual flower heads are 2 to 3 mm high. The disk flowers are mostly perfect. The ray flowers are pistillate.

Leaves The leaves are lanceolate, 3-nerved, tapered to each end, and rough above. The lower leaves are smaller and sessile, or nearly so.

Use or Importance This goldenrod may be used to make a mildly stimulating tea.

Habitat Common in a variety of open habitats: prairies, fields, roadsides, etc.

Distribution in Illinois

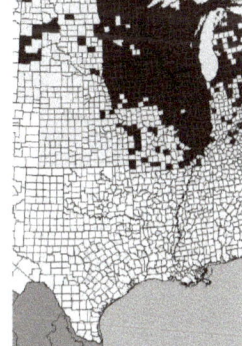

Distribution in central USA

Group D. Leaves simple, alternate.

STIFF GOLDENROD
Solidago rigida L.

STIFF GOLDENROD
Solidago rigida L.

Latin, *solido*, to make whole; in allusion to the reputed healing qualities of these perennial herbs.

Family Asteraceae, or Aster Family

Season and Stature Stiff Goldenrod is a native perennial recognized by its broad, flat-topped inflorescence. It attains a height of over one meter. It flowers during the Fall.

Flowers The goldenrod flowers are like miniature asters and are all yellow. They are arranged in an inflorescence which is about 15 cm across and more or less flat across the top.

Leaves Stiff, rough textured leaves are alternately arranged on the stem. The leaves on the lower part of the plant are oblong and have short petioles. The upper leaves are lance-olate and are sessile. There are also longer basal leaves, which overwinter.

Use or Importance Stiff Goldenrod is more palatable than other members of the goldenrod group but it is still infrequently grazed. It behaves in prairies as an invader, i.e., it tends to increase in abundance in pastures when more palatable plants have been weakened by grazing.

Habitat Prairies, dry woods.

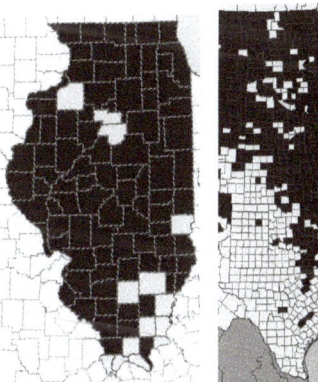
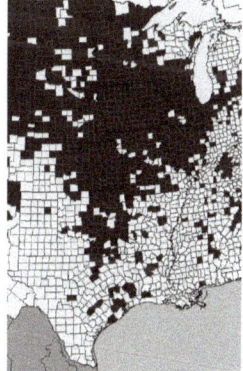

Distribution in Illinois   *Distribution in central USA*

Group D. Leaves simple, alternate.

HEATH ASTER
Symphyotrichum ericoides (L.) Nesom

HEATH ASTER

D

Symphyotrichum ericoides (L.) Nesom

From the Greek *symphyos*, (growing together) and *thrix* (hair), referring to the hair-like flowers.

Synonym *Aster ericoides* L.

Family Asteraceae, or Aster Family

Season and Stature Heath, or Frost Aster is a native, warm-season, late Summer and Fall blooming species. It attains a height up to 90 cm.

Flowers The many white heads are slightly less than one cm wide. The heads are composed of white rays surrounding yellow disk flowers. Small green leaves are borne on the stalks bearing the heads.

Leaves The leaves are small and linear to lanceolate. They are densely covered with short hairs.

Use or Importance This plant has some importance because of its soil binding quality. It is not an important forage plant except when it is very young.

Habitat Dry, open areas, from woods to prairies and fields.

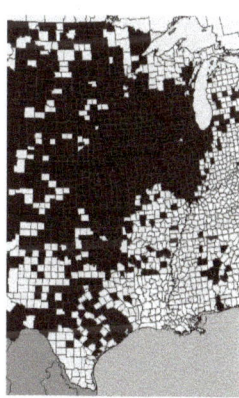

Distribution in Illinois   Distribution in central USA

Group D. Leaves simple, alternate.

SMOOTH ASTER

D

Symphyotrichum laeve (L.) A.&D. Löve

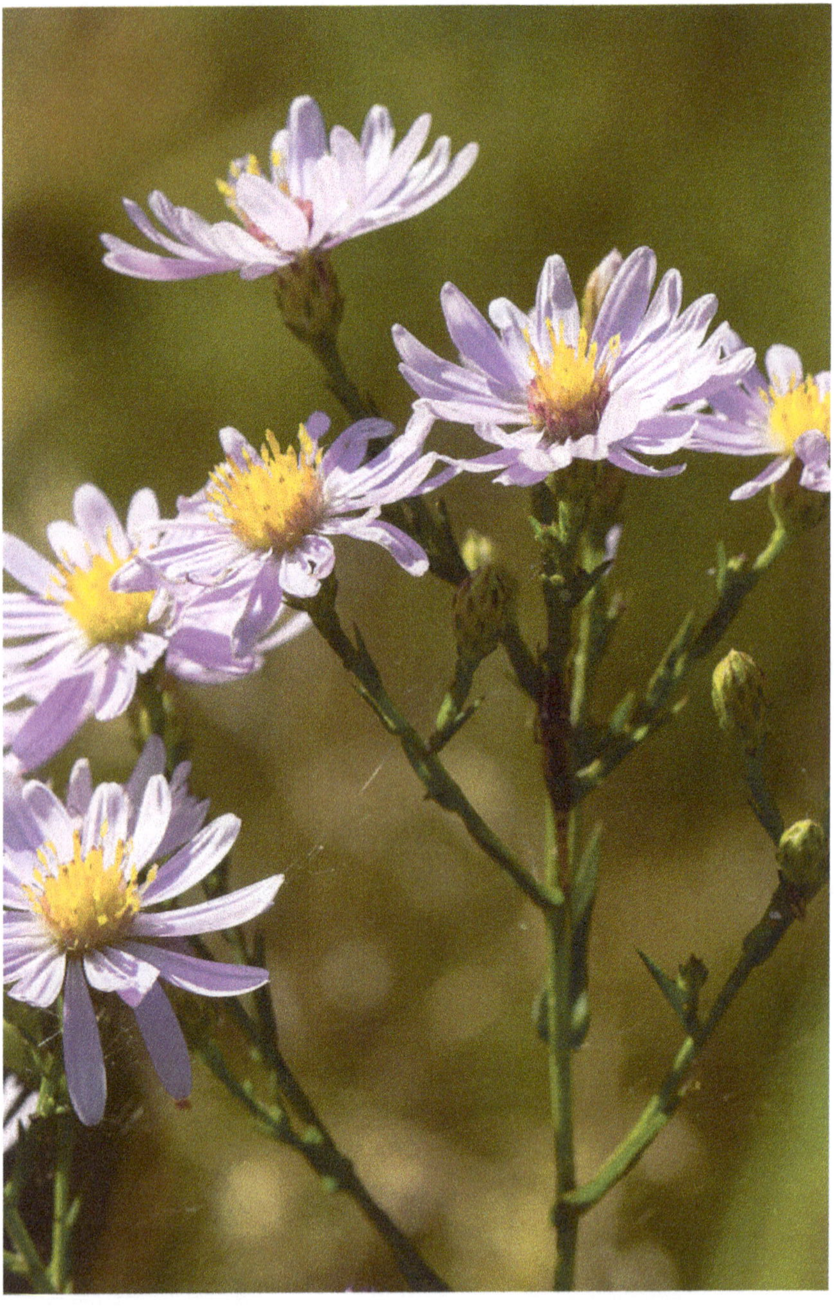

SMOOTH ASTER

Symphyotrichum laeve (L.) A.&D. Löve

From the Greek *symphyos*, (growing together) and *thrix* (hair), referring to the hair-like flowers.

Synonym *Aster laevis* L.

Family Asteraceae, or Aster Family

Season and Stature The Smooth Aster is a warm-season perennial reaching a height of one meter or more. It blooms during the Fall.

Flowers The heads are numerous, with 15 to 30 blue or violet rays. The heads are up to 2.5 cm wide.

Leaves The leaves are smooth, the upper leaves sessile, usually cordate-clasping, lanceolate, oblong-lanceolate, acute or obtuse, up to 10 cm long, and to 2 cm wide. The basal leaves are gradually narrowed into winged petioles.

Use or Importance Smooth Aster is easily grown in the native plant garden.

Habitat Moist or dry prairies, woods.

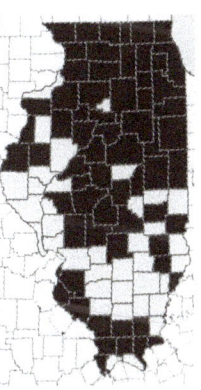

Distribution in Illinois

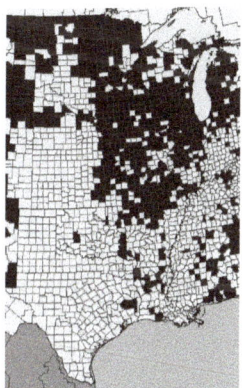

Distribution in central USA

Group D. Leaves simple, alternate.

NEW ENGLAND ASTER
Symphyotrichum novae-angliae (L.) Nesom

NEW ENGLAND ASTER

Symphyotrichum novae-angliae (L.) Nesom

Synonym *Aster novae-angliae* L.

Family Asteraceae, or Aster Family

From the Greek *symphyos*, (growing together) and *thrix* (hair), referring to the hair-like flowers.

Season and Stature New England Aster is a handsome warm-season perennial which grows to a height of one meter or more. It blooms during the Summer and Fall.

Flowers Each head, which is up to 2.5 cm wide, has a yellow disk surrounded by up to 100 narrow, bright purple rays. There are several heads in a terminal cluster.

Leaves All the leaves are heart-shaped at the base and clasp the stem. They are rough to the touch and have no teeth along the margins.

Use or Importance The colorful flowers of this species add beauty to the prairie, and are popular in gardens as well.

Habitat Woods and prairies.

Distribution in Illinois

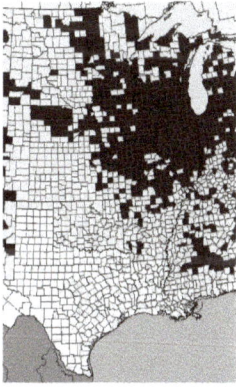

Distribution in central USA

Group D. Leaves simple, alternate.

AROMATIC ASTER
Symphyotrichum oblongifolium (Nutt.) Nesom

AROMATIC ASTER

Symphyotrichum oblongifolium (Nutt.) Nesom

Synonym *Aster oblongifolius* Nutt.

Family Asteraceae, or Aster Family

From the Greek *symphyos*, (growing together) and *thrix* (hair), referring to the hair-like flowers.

Season and Stature This late blooming aster is a native, warm-season perennial which grows to 70 cm high. It flowers from August to October.

Flowers The several heads are about 2.5 cm wide, subtended by bracts which are linear-oblong, glandular, and aromatic. The rays are rose-purple, and number between 20 and 30.

Leaves Oblong-lanceolate, sessile to partly clasping, and rough on both sides; 3 to 6 cm long.

Use or Importance Aromatic Aster is palatable to livestock when young, and behaves as a decreaser when the prairie is grazed. The plant has been grown in native plant gardens for its attractive flowers.

Habitat Upland prairies.

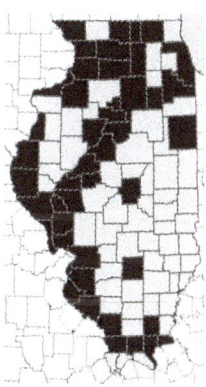

Distribution in Illinois

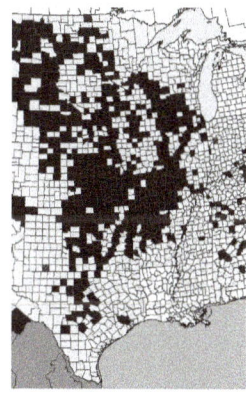

Distribution in central USA

SKY-BLUE ASTER
Symphyotrichum oolentangiense (Riddell) Nesom

SKY-BLUE ASTER

Symphyotrichum oolentangiense (Riddell) Nesom

Synonym *Aster azureus* Lindl.

Family Asteraceae, or Aster Family

From the Greek *symphyos*, (growing together) and *thrix* (hair), referring to the hair-like flowers.

Season and Stature Sky-blue Aster is a native, warm-season perennial species growing to 30 to 100 cm tall. It blooms during the Fall, from August to October.

Flowers The heads are numerous and about 5 mm high. The rays, which are about 5 mm long, are bright blue and vary in number from 10 to about 20.

Leaves Thick, entire, and rough on both sides. The basal and lower stem leaves are cordate and ovate, and from 5 to 15 cm long; they have slender petioles. The upper leaves are smaller and have much shorter petioles.

Use or Importance This blue-flowered aster is attractive and can be grown in the native plant garden. Sky-blue Aster decreases under grazing.

Habitat Both dry and moist prairies; often found along the border between the prairie and woodland.

 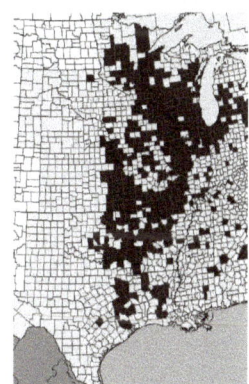

Distribution in Illinois *Distribution in central USA*

Group D. Leaves simple, alternate.

SILKY ASTER
Symphyotrichum sericeum (Vent.) Nesom

SILKY ASTER

Symphyotrichum sericeum (Vent.) Nesom

Synonym *Aster sericeus* Vent.

Family Asteraceae, or Aster Family

From the Greek *symphyos*, (growing together) and *thrix* (hair), referring to the hair-like flowers.

Season and Stature The Silky Aster, also called Silvery Aster, is a native, warm-season perennial. It attains a height up to 60 cm. It blooms during the Fall.

Flowers Silky Aster has attractive, lavender-purple or violet flowers. It has numerous heads, each one about 3 cm wide, with the rays per head numbering from 15 to 25.

Leaves The stem leaves are sessile, broadest at the base, oblong, and entire. The surfaces of the leaves are covered with a dense silvery, silky pubescence.

Use or Importance The plant decreases under grazing, hence its presence or absence helps indicate the condition of the prairie under the influence of grazing use.

Habitat Most dry habitats, including prairies and woods.

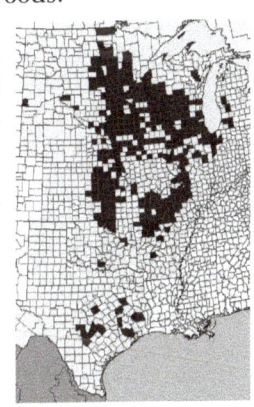

Distribution in Illinois   Distribution in central USA

Group D. Leaves simple, alternate.

GROUP E

Rattlesnake Master (*Eryngium yuccifolium*), see p. 217

GROUP E

Leaves long and narrow, at least ten times longer than broad; leaves with parallel veins; flowers showy, yellow, lavender, purple, blue, orange, or white.

WILD HYACINTH (*Camassia scilloides*), p. 215
RATTLESNAKE MASTER (*Eryngium yuccifolium*), p. 217
YELLOW STAR-GRASS (*Hypoxis hirsuta*), p. 219
ZIGZAG IRIS (*Iris brevicaulis*), p. 221
VIRGINIA BLUE FLAG (*Iris virginica*), p. 223
TURK'S-CAP LILY (*Lilium michiganense*), p. 225
WESTERN LILY (*Lilium philadelphicum*), p. 227
NARROW-LEAVED BLUE-EYED GRASS (*Sisyrinchium angustifolium*), p. 229
PRAIRIE SPIDERWORT (*Tradescantia bracteata*), p. 231
SPIDERWORT (*Tradescantia ohiensis*), p. 233
COMMON SPIDERWORT (*Tradescantia virginiana*), p. 235

WILD HYACINTH
Camassia scilloides (Raf.) Cory

WILD HYACINTH

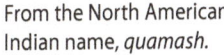

Camassia scilloides (Raf.) Cory

From the North American Indian name, *quamash*.

Family Agavaceae, or Century-Plant Family

Season and Stature Wild Hyacinth is a native, cool-season perennial, formerly classified as belonging to the Liliaceae, or Lily Family. It attains a height up to 60 cm. It flowers during the Spring.

Flowers There are 10 to 12 (or more) flowers at the ends of slender flower stalks. The perianth is 6-parted and pale blue; they are about 20 mm long. There are six stamens.

Leaves All leaves of the plant are basal, smooth, and up to 30 cm long and about 1.5 cm wide.

Use or Importance Wild Hyacinth may be grown in the garden by planting its bulbs.

Habitat Prairies and open woods.

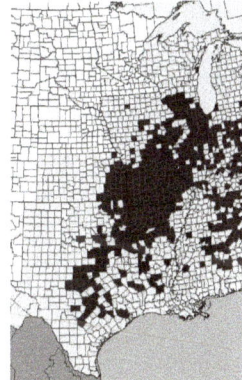

Distribution in Illinois   Distribution in central USA

Group E. Leaves long and narrow, with parallel veins. Flowers showy, yellow, lavender, purple, blue, orange, or white.

RATTLESNAKE MASTER
Eryngium yuccifolium Michx.

RATTLESNAKE MASTER

Eryngium yuccifolium Michx.   The Greek name for these herbs.

Family Apiaceae, or Carrot Family

Season and Stature A native, warm-season perennial which grows to a height of one meter or more. It flowers during the Summer.

Flowers The flowers are borne in thistle-like, spherical heads up to 2.5 cm in diameter. The flowers are small, with 5 sepals, 5 petals, and 5 stamens. The ovary is inferior.

Leaves The leaves are stiffish, bayonet-shaped with teeth along the margins, and look much like those of yucca, from which its Latin name is derived.

Use or Importance New growth of Rattlesnake Master is palatable and nutritious. It is readily grazed and thus behaves as a decreaser. The common name indicates the early settlers thought the plant had use in treatment of rattlesnake bite (this was unfounded). The plant can be dried and used in indoor winter decorations.

Habitat This species occurs in both prairies and woods.

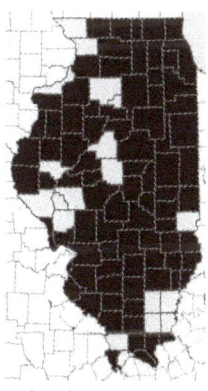
Distribution in Illinois
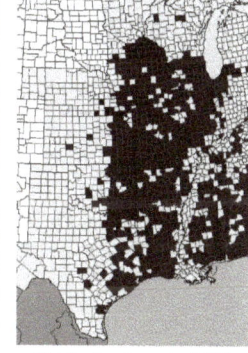
Distribution in central USA

Group E. Leaves long and narrow, with parallel veins. Flowers showy, yellow, lavender, purple, blue, orange, or white.

YELLOW STAR-GRASS
Hypoxis hirsuta (L.) Coville

YELLOW STAR-GRASS
Hypoxis hirsuta (L.) Coville

Gr. *hypo*, under; *oxys*, sharp; in allusion to the form of the base of the seed capsule.

Family Hypoxidaceae, or Yellow Star-Grass Family

Season and Stature Yellow Star-Grass is a native, short perennial, formerly classified as belonging to the Liliaceae, or Lily Family. It begins growth during the Spring and usually flowers into May and June. The plant grows to about 15 cm tall.

Flowers The one to several flowers are on slender scapes in a simple, umbellate fashion. There are six yellow perianth parts, six stamens, and a three-parted inferior ovary.

Leaves The leaves are basal, linear and grass-like, and somewhat hairy. The leaves are mostly longer than the scapes.

Use or Importance Yellow Star-Grass has no great importance, although it is an attractive spring wildflower due to its diminutive stature and bright yellow flowers.

Habitat Dry situations, including woods, bluff-tops, and prairies.

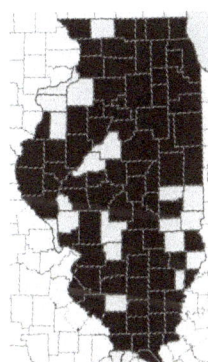

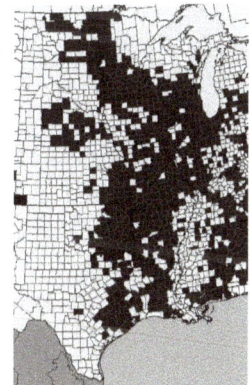

Distribution in Illinois   *Distribution in central USA*

ZIGZAG IRIS
Iris brevicaulis Raf.

ZIGZAG IRIS

Iris brevicaulis Raf.

Perennials named for the Greek goddess of the rainbow.

Family Iridaceae, or Iris Family

Season and Stature Zigzag Iris is a cool-season, native perennial. It attains a height of 20 to 40 cm, and blooms during the Spring.

Flowers The flowers are a deep blue color and are borne near ground level. The perianth parts are 7 to 9 cm long and 2.5 to 3 cm wide. The flowers are subtended by subequal bracts which are up to 5 cm long.

Leaves The leaves are rather soft. They may reach a length of 60 cm with a width of 3 cm.

Use or Importance This is a very attractive iris, and is well adapted to garden culture.

Habitat Swampy woods and in wet prairies.

Distribution in Illinois

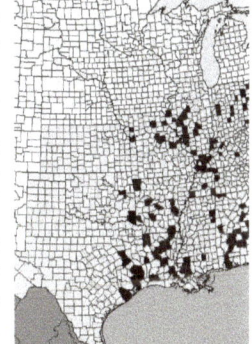

Distribution in central USA

Group E. Leaves long and narrow, with parallel veins. Flowers showy, yellow, lavender, purple, blue, orange, or white.

VIRGINIA BLUE FLAG

E

Iris virginica L.

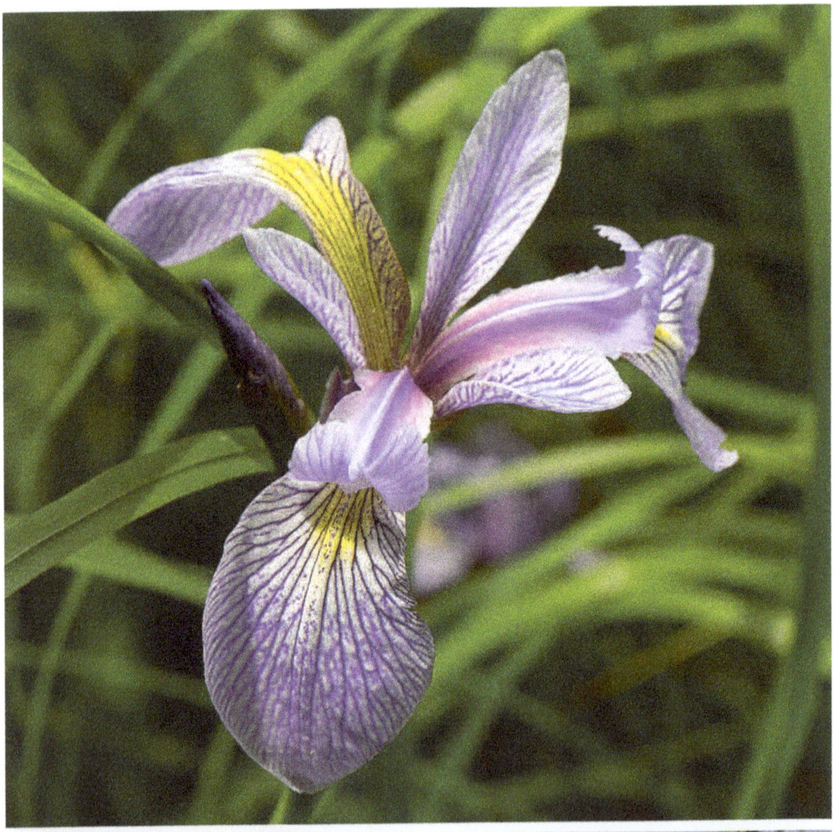

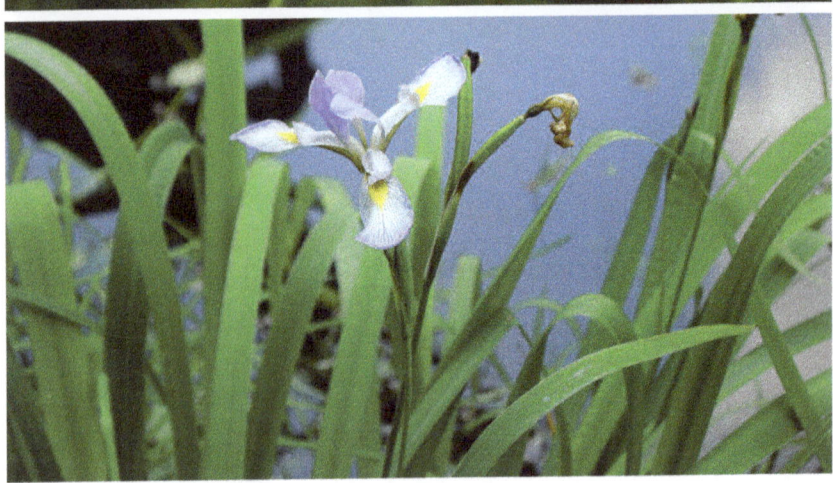

VIRGINIA BLUE FLAG

Iris virginica L.

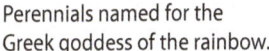

Perennials named for the Greek goddess of the rainbow.

Synonym *Iris shrevii* Small

Family Iridaceae, or Iris Family

Season and Stature Virginia Blue Flag is a native perennial reaching a height of one meter. It flowers during May and June.

Flowers The blue flowers are up to 8 cm wide, and have 3 stamens. The ovary is inferior.

Leaves The leaves are sword-shaped and up to one meter long and up to 3 cm broad.

Use or Importance Sometimes cultivated in flower gardens.

Habitat In a variety of wet situations, including low prairies.

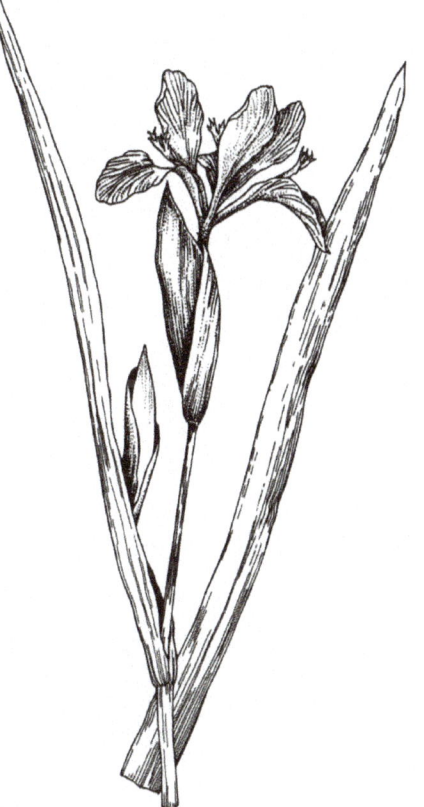

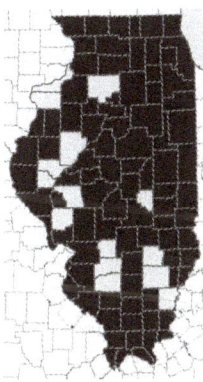

Distribution in Illinois

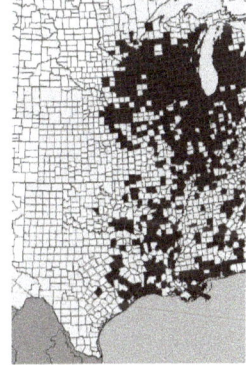

Distribution in central USA

Group E. Leaves long and narrow, with parallel veins. Flowers showy, yellow, lavender, purple, blue, orange, or white.

TURK'S-CAP LILY
Lilium michiganense Farw.

TURK'S-CAP LILY

Lilium michiganense Farw.

The Latin name akin to Gr. *leirion*, the madonna-lily.

Family Liliaceae, or Lily Family

Season and Stature Turk's-cap Lily is a Summer-blooming plant which grows up to 2 meters tall. It grows from an underground bulb.

Flowers The flowers are orange or orange-yellow with brownish-purplish spots. The flowers are from one (rarely) to several and are borne on long peduncles. The perianth segments are 5 to 10 cm long, lanceolate, and strongly recurved.

Leaves The lanceolate leaves are smooth, tapering at both ends, 5 to 15 cm long, up to 4 cm wide, and grouped in clusters of 3 to 8.

Use or Importance This lily is cultivated for its handsome flowers.

Habitat In a variety of rather moist habitats, including prairies and woods.

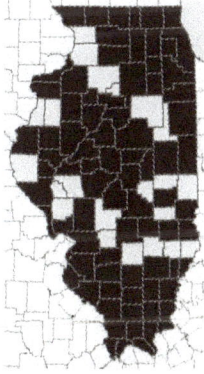

Distribution in Illinois

Distribution in central USA

Group E. Leaves long and narrow, with parallel veins. Flowers showy, yellow, lavender, purple, blue, orange, or white.

WESTERN LILY
Lilium philadelphicum L.

WESTERN LILY

Lilium philadelphicum L.

The Latin name akin to Gr. *leirion*, the madonna-lily.

Family Liliaceae, or Lily Family

Season and Stature Western Lily is a native warm-season plant belonging to the family Liliaceae. It attains a height of up to one meter and blooms during June or July.

Flowers The flowers are orange to orange-red and very striking in their beauty. There are 1 to 5 flowers on stout pedicels. The perianth parts are purple spotted within.

Leaves The uppermost leaves are whorled, while the lowermost leaves are alternate. The leaves are narrowly lanceolate, up to 10 cm long and up to 1 cm wide.

Use or Importance Because of its beauty and bulb habit, this species has possibilities for cultivation in gardens, as well as in restored or artificial prairies.

Habitat Dry prairies and open woodlands.

Distribution in Illinois

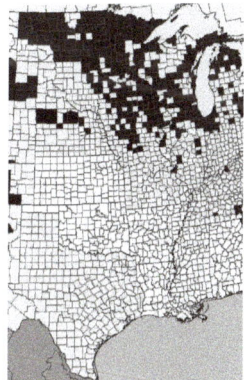

Distribution in central USA

Group E. Leaves long and narrow, with parallel veins. Flowers showy, yellow, lavender, purple, blue, orange, or white.

NARROW-LEAVED BLUE-EYED GRASS E
Sisyrinchium angustifolium P. Mill.

NARROW-LEAVED BLUE-EYED GRASS E

Sisyrinchium angustifolium P. Mill. The ancient Greek name for another plant.

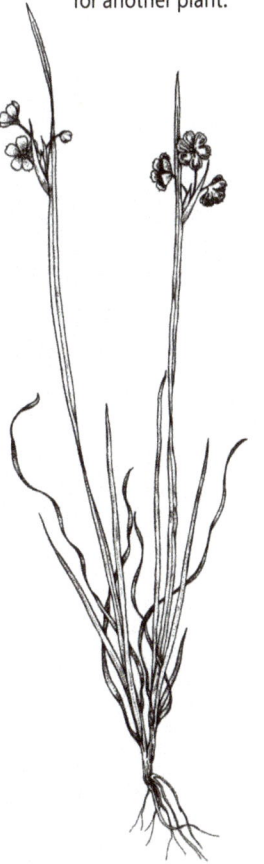

Family Iridaceae, or Iris Family

Season and Stature Narrow-leaved Blue-Eyed Grass is a native, perennial, cool-season herb. It attains a height of 10 to 60 cm and blooms during the Spring.

Flowers The color of the flowers is deep to pale violet-blue. There are six perianth parts, each less than 1 cm long. The ovary is inferior. The flower is subtended by a green spathe.

Leaves The leaves are half the height of the stem (to slightly longer), and to 2 mm or more wide. They are produced from winged stems.

Use or Importance The plants have underground rootstocks which apparently have been eaten by pigs, as the plants also have the name "pigroot."

Habitat In a variety of habitats, including nearly all prairie types.

Distribution in Illinois
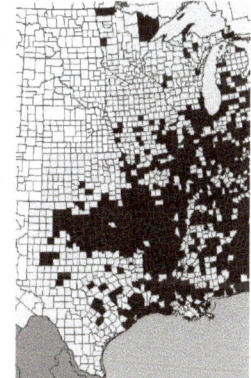
Distribution in central USA

Group E. Leaves long and narrow, with parallel veins. Flowers showy, yellow, lavender, purple, blue, orange, or white.   229

PRAIRIE SPIDERWORT
Tradescantia bracteata Small

PRAIRIE SPIDERWORT
Tradescantia bracteata Small

Perennial herbs named for John Tradescant (d. 1638), gardener to King Charles I.

Family Commelinaceae, or Spiderwort Family

Season and Stature Prairie Spiderwort is a cool-season perennial, growing to a height of 35 to 45 cm. It blooms in Spring.

Flowers The flowers are borne in terminal cymes subtended by two long, leaf-like bracts which are broader than the leaves. The calyx is 3-parted, green, symmetrical, and glandular-viscid. The 3 petals are rose or magenta colored.

Leaves The leaves and stems are smooth; leaves are 10 to 20 cm long, and 0.5 to 1.5 cm wide.

Use or Importance Most spiderworts can be grown in gardens.

Habitat Sandy prairies. Uncommon in Illinois, becoming more common in the Great Plains.

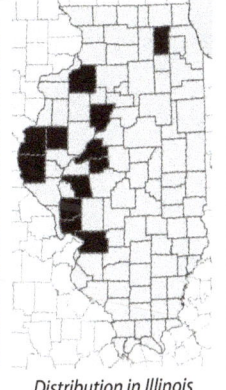
Distribution in Illinois
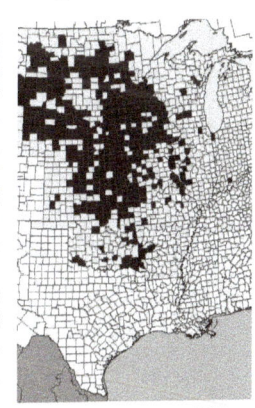
Distribution in central USA

Group E. Leaves long and narrow, with parallel veins. Flowers showy, yellow, lavender, purple, blue, orange, or white.

SPIDERWORT
Tradescantia ohiensis Raf.

SPIDERWORT
Tradescantia ohiensis Raf.

Perennial herbs named for John Tradescant (d. 1638), gardener to King Charles I.

Family Commelinaceae, or Spiderwort Family

Season and Stature Spiderwort is a cool-season perennial. It reaches a height of 20 to 60 cm, and flowers during the Spring.

Flowers The three petals of the flowers are deep blue to purplish-blue. The green sepals are smooth or with a tuft of non-glandular hairs at the tip.

Leaves The smooth leaves are long and slender, up to 45 cm long and to 3.5 cm wide.

Use or Importance This species is sometimes cultivated for its attractive flowers.

Habitat In most prairie types, especially the tallgrass prairie. It also grows along the margins of woods, and along roadsides and gravel or cinder-banked railroad rights-of-way.

Distribution in Illinois

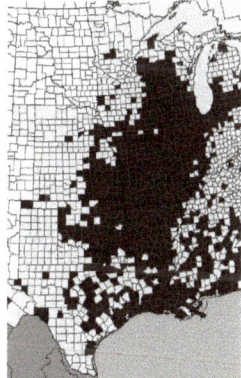

Distribution in central USA

COMMON SPIDERWORT
Tradescantia virginiana L.

COMMON SPIDERWORT

Tradescantia virginiana L.

Family Commelinaceae, or Spiderwort Family

Perennial herbs named for John Tradescant (d. 1638), gardener to King Charles I.

Season and Stature Common Spiderwort is a cool-season perennial which may reach a height of 30 cm. It blooms during the Spring.

Flowers The flowers, which are usually blue, are borne in terminal cymes subtended by two long, leaf-like bracts. The three sepals are green and without glands. There are also three petals.

Leaves The leaves are smooth, and up to 25 cm long and to nearly 2 cm wide.

Use or Importance A favorite in gardens because of its attractive flowers.

Habitat Prairies and woodlands.

Distribution in Illinois

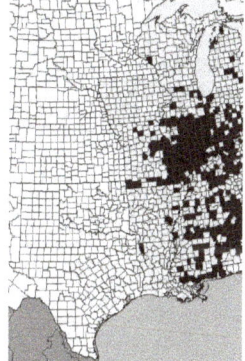

Distribution in central USA

Group E. Leaves long and narrow, with parallel veins. Flowers showy, yellow, lavender, purple, blue, orange, or white.

GROUP F

SIDE-OATS GRAMA (*Bouteloua curtipendula*), see p. 241

GROUP F

Leaves long and narrow, at least ten times longer than broad; leaves with parallel veins; flowers inconspicuous, green or brown or straw-colored, without petals.

BIG BLUESTEM (*Andropogon gerardii*), p. 239
SIDE-OATS GRAMA (*Bouteloua curtipendula*), p. 241
PENNSYLVANIA SEDGE (*Carex pensylvanica*), p. 243
MEAD'S SEDGE (*Carex meadii*), p. 245
SCRIBNER'S PANIC GRASS (*Dichanthelium oligosanthes*), p. 247
NODDING WILD RYE (*Elymus canadensis*), p. 249
NEEDLEGRASS (*Hesperostipa spartea*), p. 251
LITTLE WILD BARLEY (*Hordeum pusillum*), p. 253
PATH RUSH (*Juncus tenuis*), p. 255
TORREY'S RUSH (*Juncus torreyi*), p. 257
JUNE GRASS (*Koeleria macrantha*), p. 259
WITCH GRASS (*Panicum capillare*), p. 261
SWITCHGRASS (*Panicum virgatum*), p. 263
KENTUCKY BLUEGRASS (*Poa pratensis*), p. 265
LITTLE BLUESTEM (*Schizachyrium scoparium*), p. 267
INDIAN GRASS (*Sorghastrum nutans*), p. 269
TALL DROPSEED (*Sporobolus compositus*), p. 271
SAND DROPSEED (*Sporobolus cryptandrus*), p. 273
PRAIRIE DROPSEED (*Sporobolus heterolepis*), p. 275
PRAIRIE CORDGRASS (*Sporobolus michauxianus*), p. 277
EASTERN GAMA GRASS (*Tripsacum dactyloides*), p. 279
SIX-WEEKS FESCUE (*Vulpia octoflora*), p. 281

BIG BLUESTEM
Andropogon gerardii Vitman

BIG BLUESTEM

Andropogon gerardii Vitman

From Gr. *aner*, a man; *pogon*, a beard; in reference to the hairs on the spikelets of some species of these grasses.

Family Poaceae, or Grass Family

Season and Stature Big Bluestem is a native, warm-season perennial tall grass. It begins growth in late April and flowers in late summer, growing to 2.5 meters (or sometimes more).

Flowers Spikelets are borne in pairs, one sessile, one pedicelled. The inflorescence is 3-branched, each of which is a raceme. Because of this, it has been called "turkey foot" bluestem.

Leaves The lower leaf sheath of young growth has long hairs. The young shoots are somewhat flattened and the young *culms* (stems in grasses) are oval in cross-section.

Use or Importance A chief component of the original prairie, used for grazing or as a hay meadow. It decreases under heavy grazing (prairies heavily grazed usually degenerate to lower condition because of competitive benefit to less palatable species).

Habitat Big Bluestem is a lowland dominant. It grows in moist soil, sometimes on the lower slopes; less often on drier uplands.

Note The predominance of this species caused the eastern, humid prairies to be called "bluestem prairie," or "tall grass prairie," and is a dominant species in the True Prairie. In Mixed Prairie it is found in moist ravines and valley bottoms.

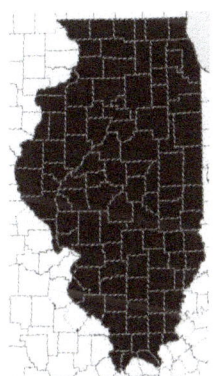

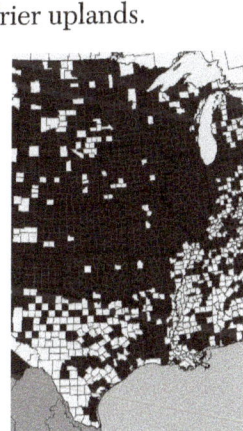

Distribution in Illinois   *Distribution in central USA*

SIDE-OATS GRAMA
Bouteloua curtipendula (Michx.) Torr.

SIDE-OATS GRAMA

Bouteloua curtipendula (Michx.) Torr. Named for Claudio and Esteban Boutelou, 19th century Spanish brothers and gardeners.

Family Poaceae, or Grass Family

Season and Stature Side-oats Grama is a warm-season, tufted perennial; typically found on the prairie as scattered plants rather than forming a pure stand. When in flower in Summer, plants may grow to 90 cm tall.

Flowers The spikelets are borne on simple racemes, arranged on one side of the rachis. It is from this arrangement of spikelets that the plant takes its name "Side-Oats." The anthers are a bright red-purple color.

Leaves The leaf blades are flat, up to one cm wide, and often have dead, curly tips (the dead tip may be about 1/4 to 1/2 the length of the blade). The leaves often have dark, pustule-like marks. Along both the margins of the leaves are hairs which have a bulbous gland at their base (magnification helps in seeing this feature).

Use or Importance Side-oats Grama is a palatable and nutritious grass.

Habitat Side-oats Grama occupies all manner of upland sites from lower slopes to the brow of the hill, or the breaks near the crest. It may occupy deep or shallow soil.

Note This species ranges widely over the grasslands east of the Rocky Mountains. It is more common in the drier Mixed Prairie than in True Prairie, especially among the tall grasses where it does not tolerate shading.

Distribution in Illinois

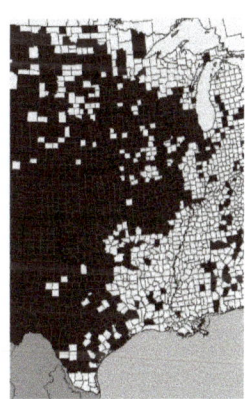

Distribution in central USA

Group F. Leaves long and narrow, with parallel veins. Flowers inconspicuous, green or brown or straw-colored, without petals.

MEAD'S SEDGE
Carex meadii Dewey

MEAD'S SEDGE

Carex meadii Dewey — The classical Latin name.

F

Family Cyperaceae, or Sedge Family

Season and Stature Mead's Sedge is a native species which attains a height of about 50 cm. It flowers during the Spring and early Summer.

Flowers The staminate spike is borne on a long stalk and is densely crowded with pollen-producing flowers. The 1-3 oblong-cylindric pistillate spikes are up to 2 cm long and up to 5 mm across.

Leaves The leaves of the sedge are smooth, flat and measure 3-5 mm across.

Use or Importance This sedge has minimal importance as a forage plant.

Habitat Mead's Sedge grows in moist soil or prairies and meadows throughout most of Illinois and the Midwest.

Note Sedges are a large genus of plants in Illinois, and often difficult to identify. In prairies, sedges are most likely to occur in seasonally wet depressions, or in true wetlands such as pond edges and marshes.

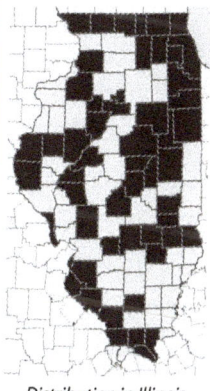

Distribution in Illinois

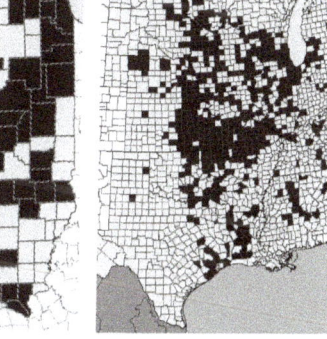

Distribution in central USA

Group F. Leaves long and narrow, with parallel veins. Flowers inconspicuous, green or brown or straw-colored, without petals.

PENNSYLVANIA SEDGE

F

Carex pensylvanica Lam.

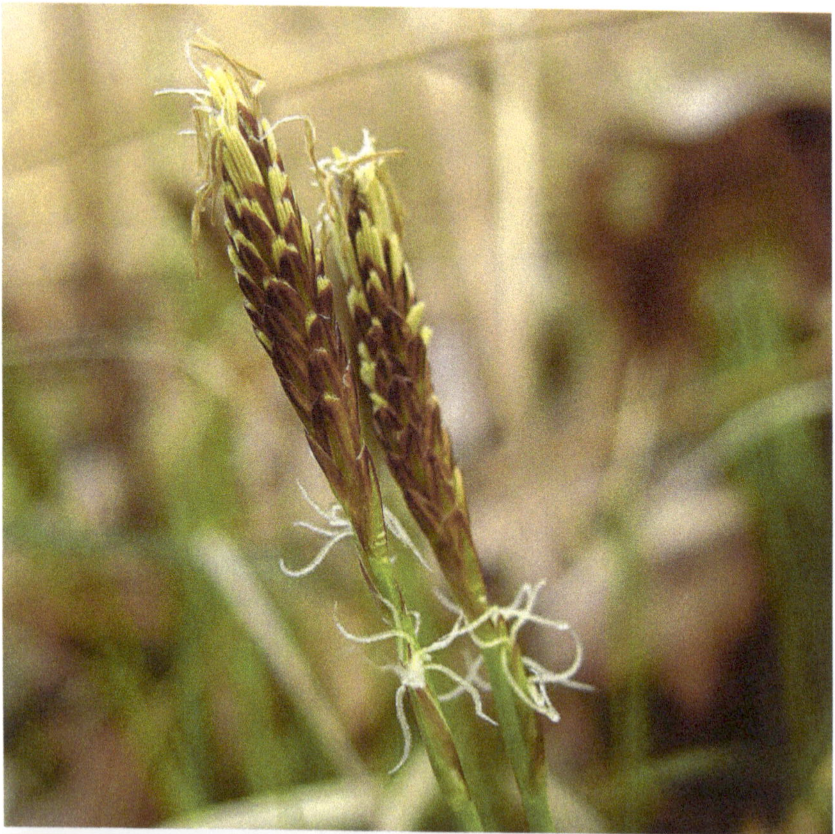

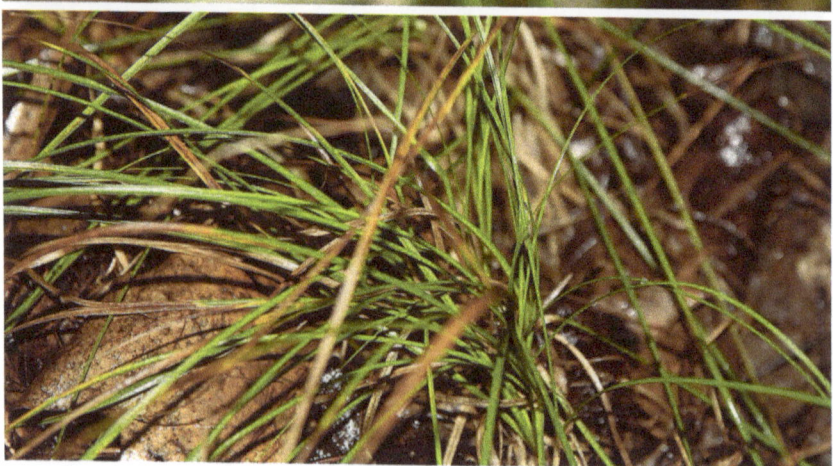

PENNSYLVANIA SEDGE

Carex pensylvanica Lam. The classical Latin name.

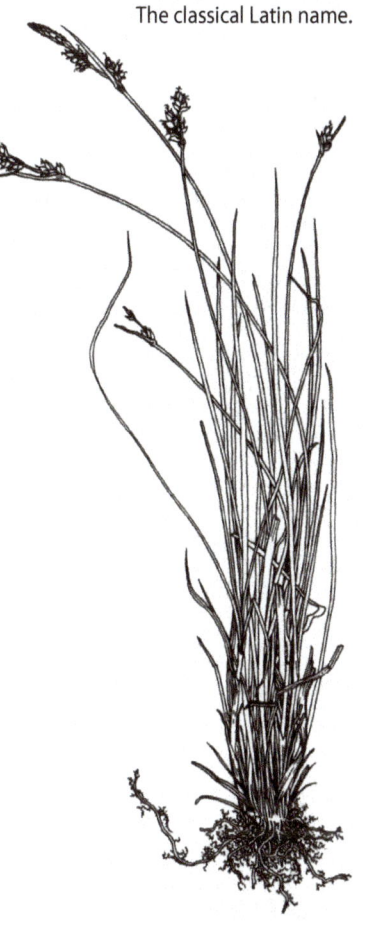

Family Cyperaceae, or Sedge Family

Season and Stature Pennsylvania Sedge grows in small tufts up to 30 cm tall. It is a native sedge which blooms during the Spring.

Flowers The staminate spike is reddish-brown and up to 2 cm long (see photo, p. 244). It is usually borne on a short stalk. The 1–4 ovoid pistillate spikes are up to 1.2 cm long and sessile or on very short stalks.

Leaves Leaves of Pennsylvania Sedge are very slender, reaching a width of only 3 mm (see photo, p. 244).

Use or Importance To a small extent, this sedge is used for forage.

Habitat In dry, usually sandy soil of open woods and prairies.

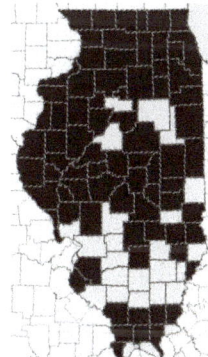
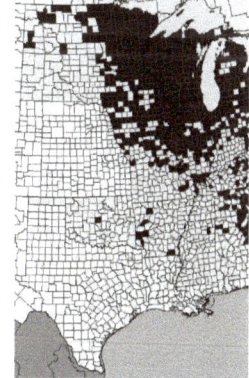

Distribution in Illinois *Distribution in central USA*

Group F. Leaves long and narrow, with parallel veins. Flowers inconspicuous, green or brown or straw-colored, without petals.

SCRIBNER'S PANIC GRASS F
Dichanthelium oligosanthes (J.A. Schultes) Gould

SCRIBNER'S PANIC GRASS

Dichanthelium oligosanthes (J.A. Schultes) Gould

From the Greek *dicha* (twice or bifid) and *anthelion*, (diminutive of anthos or flower).

Synonym *Panicum oligosanthes* J.A. Schultes

Family Poaceae, or Grass Family

Season and Stature This species, unlike most species of *Dichanthelium*, is a cool-season grass. It is a native, tufted, perennial of low stature, growing to only 20 to 30 cm. Flowering is in late spring with vegetative growth in early spring. During fall and winter, new, small leaves form a rosette on the ground.

Flowers The panicles are short and bear spikelets which are single-flowered and produce fruits which are 3 to 4 mm long.

Leaves Leaf blades are short and pointed, up to 6 cm long, and to 2 cm wide. Fine hairs are present on the undersides of the leaves and on the leaf base and the sheath.

Use or Importance Provides limited forage for grazing animals. The plant decreases under heavy grazing of prairies.

Habitat Dry prairies and open woods, usually on sandy soils..

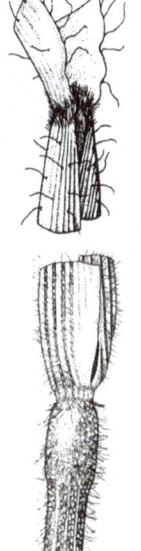

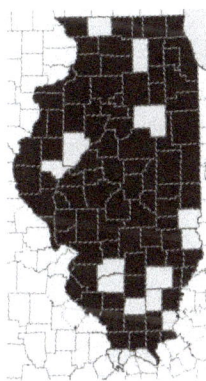
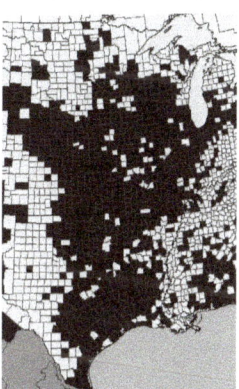

Distribution in Illinois   Distribution in central USA

Group F. Leaves long and narrow, with parallel veins. Flowers inconspicuous, green or brown or straw-colored, without petals.

NODDING WILD RYE
Elymus canadensis L.

NODDING WILD RYE

Elymus canadensis L.

From the Greek name for a kind of grass.

Family Poaceae, or Grass Family

Season and Stature This moderately tall grass, grows to about one meter tall. It is a cool-season, perennial grass forming a weak sod. It begins growth in March or April and matures by July. It may become green at the base of the plant and renew growth during the Fall.

Flowers The spikes are dense, usually curving or nodding, 10 to 25 cm long, and 2 or more cm wide. The spikelets are 2- to 7-flowered. The lemmas usually have long curving awns which give the spikes a bushy look.

Leaves Green early in the season and again in the fall. The leaves are one cm or more in width, and clasp the culm by means of auricles which extend part way around the culm.

Use or Importance Because of its early growth, it is sought by all classes of livestock, and is considered a highly palatable grass. It is a decreaser in prairies which are grazed too heavily or too early in the year.

Habitat A lowland dominant, found in True Prairie in the transition from lowland to upland. Roadsides and cinder banks along railroads also provide suitable habitat.

Distribution in Illinois

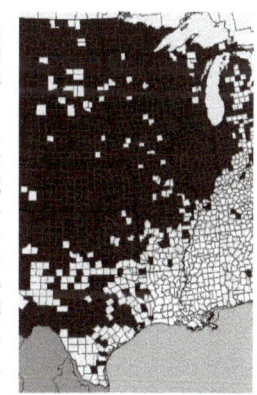

Distribution in central USA

Group F. Leaves long and narrow, with parallel veins. Flowers inconspicuous, green or brown or straw-colored, without petals.

NEEDLEGRASS
Hesperostipa spartea (Trin.) Barkworth

NEEDLEGRASS

Hesperostipa spartea (Trin.) Barkworth Gr. *stuppeion*, tow or flax; from the feathery inflorescence.

Synonym *Stipa spartea* Trin.

Family Poaceae, or Grass Family

Season and Stature Needlegrass is named for its sharp-pointed, callus-tipped fruit (and has also been called "needle and thread" due to its long awns, 10 cm or more, which resemble a thread). It is a cool-season grass of midheight (30 to 90 cm). It begins growth in April, and flowers by June. It is dormant in Summer and resumes growth in September.

Flowers The inflorescence is a narrow panicle up to 25 cm long. The fruits are from single-flowered spikelets, and fall from the glumes at maturity. The fruits have a hygroscopic awn which aids the "planting of the fruit" by its own self-induced, twisting mechanism.

Leaves The plant grows in small tufts 6 to 10 cm in diameter. The leaves are ribbed on the underside; the upper surface is smooth.

Use or Importance Needlegrass is known as a hard grass because of its high proportion of fiber. Despite this, Needlegrass is palatable, particularly when young, and due to its early availability as a cool-season grass. Needlegrass is a decreaser in grazed prairies.

Habitat Dry prairies and woodlands, soils usually sandy.

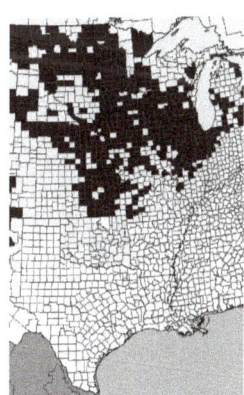

Distribution in Illinois   *Distribution in central USA*

Group F. Leaves long and narrow, with parallel veins. Flowers inconspicuous, green or brown or straw-colored, without petals. 251

LITTLE WILD BARLEY
Hordeum pusillum Nutt.

LITTLE WILD BARLEY
Hordeum pusillum Nutt.

Latin name for barley (*H. vulgare*).

Family Poaceae, or Grass Family

Season and Stature Little Wild Barley is a native, weedy, annual, cool-season, grass; plants reach a height of 30 cm (sometimes more). It flowers and produces fruit during the Spring and early Summer. The root system is shallow.

Flowers The spikes are up to 6-8 cm in length and are dense and erect. Spikelets number 3 at each joint and are awned.

Leaves Leaf blades are up to 7 cm long, flat, and somewhat rough on the upper surface.

Use or Importance Limited grazing is about the only use made of Little Wild Barley, and this occurs during Spring. When abundant, the plant serves as an indicator of overgrazed prairie or pasture.

Habitat Most often in disturbed areas within prairies, and on a wide variety of soils.

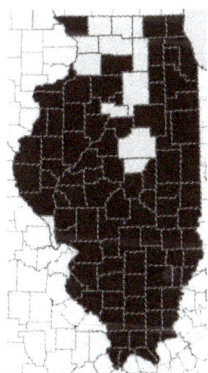

Distribution in Illinois   Distribution in central USA

Group F. Leaves long and narrow, with parallel veins. Flowers inconspicuous, green or brown or straw-colored, without petals.

PATH RUSH
Juncus tenuis Willd.

PATH RUSH

Juncus tenuis Willd.

The classical Latin name for the bulrush.

Family Juncaceae, or Rush Family

Season and Stature Path Rush is a native cool-season plant having a tufted growth and attaining a height up to 90 cm.

Flowers The inflorescence is usually exceeded by an elongated bract. The flowers are greenish-brown and up to 3 mm long. There are six stamens.

Leaves The Path Rush has basal leaves which are about half the length of the culms. The leaves are about 1 mm wide.

Use or Importance This species is called Path Rush because it often grows on the moist, compacted soil of pathways and trails.

Habitat This species grows in moist or somewhat dry soil, especially where compacted.

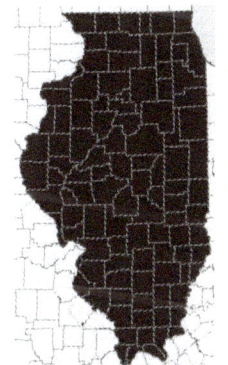

Distribution in Illinois

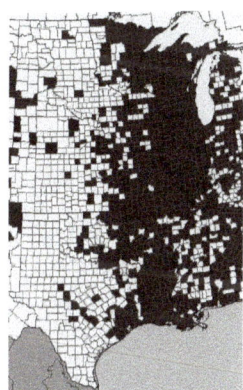

Distribution in central USA

Group F. Leaves long and narrow, with parallel veins. Flowers inconspicuous, green or brown or straw-colored, without petals.

TORREY'S RUSH
Juncus torreyi Coville

TORREY'S RUSH

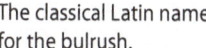

Juncus torreyi Coville

The classical Latin name for the bulrush.

Family Juncaceae, or Rush Family

Season and Stature Torrey's Rush is a native species flowering during the Summer. It attains a height up to one meter.

Flowers The inflorescence consists of 1 to 20 round heads, each about 1 cm in diameter. The inflorescence is exceeded by its lowest bract.

Leaves There are 1 to 4 leaves with stout, terete (round in cross-section) blades, up to 1 mm or more in thickness.

Use or Importance Many rushes have durable leaves and stems and have been used in basketry.

Habitat Wet soil, including moist, lowland prairies.

Distribution in Illinois

Distribution in central USA

Group F. Leaves long and narrow, with parallel veins. Flowers inconspicuous, green or brown or straw-colored, without petals.

JUNE GRASS
Koeleria macrantha (Ledeb.) J.A. Schultes

JUNE GRASS
Koeleria macrantha (Ledeb.) J.A. Schultes

Synonym *Koeleria cristata* auct. p.p. Non Pers.

Family Poaceae, or Grass Family

Named for George Ludwig Koeler, 18th century German botanist at Mainz.

Season and Stature June Grass is a native, cool-season perennial. At flowering time, with the culm and inflorescence included, it is a grass of mid-height, reaching a height of about 60 cm. It flowers during the early Summer.

Flowers At flowering time, the spikelets are densely borne in narrow or spike-like panicles up to 12 cm long. The spikelets are 2- to 4-flowered, with the glumes shorter than the spikelets. As they mature, the panicles become more open and spreading.

Leaves The leaves tend to twist or spiral and are unevenly veined. The leaves are up to 20 cm long and to 3 mm wide.

Use or Importance June Grass is a palatable species which decreases under heavy grazing of the prairies.

Habitat A medium-sized tufted species whose position in the moisture gradient is indefinite, as it may be found from lowland to dry hilltop. It is known as an 'interstitial species' because it is scattered among the other major dominants and does not form a community of its own.

Distribution in Illinois

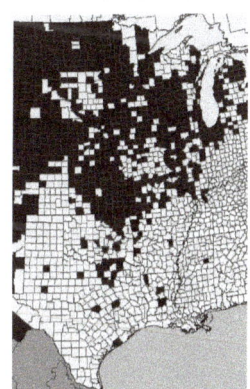

Distribution in central USA

Group F. Leaves long and narrow, with parallel veins. Flowers inconspicuous, green or brown or straw-colored, without petals.

WITCH GRASS
Panicum capillare L.

WITCH GRASS

Panicum capillare L.   The Latin name.

Family Poaceae, or Grass Family

Season and Stature Witch Grass is a native, annual, weedy grass, found where the prairie has degenerated under excessive grazing. The plant grows and flowers during the warm-season. It becomes conspicuous during the Fall when it attains a height up to 60 cm.

Flowers The panicle is from 20 to 30 cm long. It is about half as wide as long. There is a tuft of hairs at the juncture of each of the main panicle branches and the rachis. The spikelets are single-flowered. The entire panicle may break loose and blow about as a "tumbleweed" in Fall.

Leaves The plant grows in small bunches, or tufts. The leaf blades are 10 to 20 cm long and about 1 cm wide. The leaf sheath is very hairy.

Use or Importance Witch Grass serves as an indicator of the condition of prairie. It is never abundant or is seldom present in a vigorous thriving prairie. Witch Grass is not often eaten by livestock.

Habitat On a wide variety of soils. Its presence indicates poor or degenerated conditions.

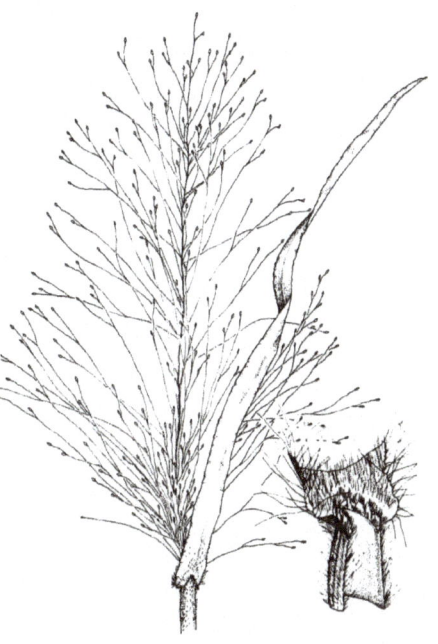

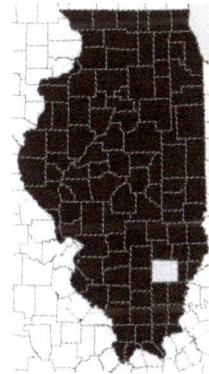
Distribution in Illinois

Distribution in central USA

Group F. Leaves long and narrow, with parallel veins. Flowers inconspicuous, green or brown or straw-colored, without petals.

SWITCHGRASS
Panicum virgatum L.

SWITCHGRASS
Panicum virgatum L.

The Latin name.

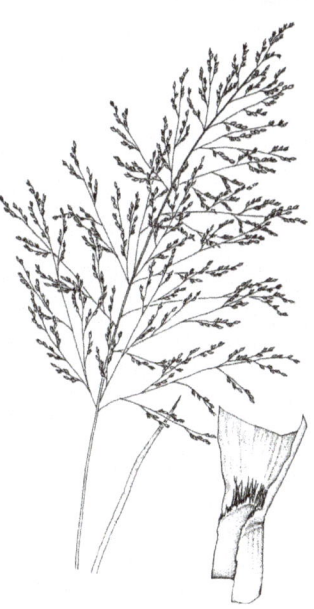

Family Poaceae, or Grass Family

Season and Stature Also called Tall Panic Grass. It is a native, warm-season, sod-forming perennial grass. It begins growth in late April or mid-May. Switchgrass may grow up to 2 meters tall, but is usually somewhat shorter than nearby plants of Big Bluestem or Indian Grass.

Flowers The well-developed panicle is often up to 60 cm long, and bears numerous fruits from 3 to 6 mm long and to 1.5 mm wide. The fruits are developed from a single-flowered spikelet. Both glumes are present and well-developed.

Leaves Persistent on the plant into winter, and are closely clustered to give the lower half of the plant a dense growth appearance. The leaves have a copious patch of hairs or dense pubescence in the form of an inverted "V" shape where the leaf joins the *culm* (stem in grasses).

Use or Importance Palatable in its early growth and readily eaten by grazing animals. It will decrease under uncontrolled or heavy grazing and should not be grazed too low to the ground. Easily established and popular for land-reclamation and prairie restoration.

Habitat Switchgrass is a lowland dominant. and grows well in moist bottomland situations, as well as somewhat drier situations.

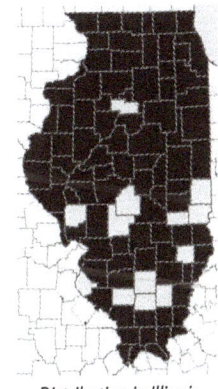

Distribution in Illinois

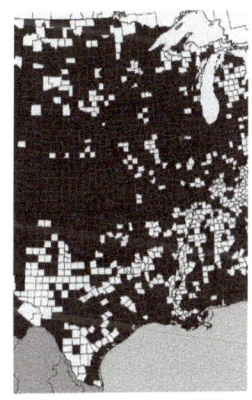

Distribution in central USA

KENTUCKY BLUEGRASS
Poa pratensis L.

KENTUCKY BLUEGRASS

Poa pratensis L.

Gr. *poa*, grass.

Family Poaceae, or Grass Family

Season and Stature Kentucky Bluegrass, although considered a non-native grass, is widely represented in prairies today, and has become thoroughly naturalized in much of the USA. In prairies, Kentucky Bluegrass is adapted to growing in the shade of the taller grasses. Bluegrass is a cool-season, sod-forming grass up to 60 cm in height.

Flowers The medium-wide panicle supports spikelets which have 2-5 flowers. The bluegrasses have a mass of cobwebby hairs at the base of the lemmas. The flowers and fruits mature in late Spring and early Summer.

Leaves The leaf blades are long, and uniformly slender to the tip where they terminate in a boat-shaped end.

Use or Importance Kentucky Bluegrass affords good early grazing. The species is palatable and nutritious and is classed as a soft grass. Under heavy grazing, prairie grasses may be replaced by Kentucky Bluegrass.

Habitat Tolerant of shade and found as an undergrowth species to the tall grasses. It occurs in a wide range of moist to dry conditions.

Distribution in Illinois

Distribution in central USA

Group F. Leaves long and narrow, with parallel veins. Flowers inconspicuous, green or brown or straw-colored, without petals.

LITTLE BLUESTEM
Schizachyrium scoparium (Michx.) Nash

LITTLE BLUESTEM
Schizachyrium scoparium (Michx.) Nash

Synonym *Andropogon scoparius* Michx.

Family Poaceae, or Grass Family

Season and Stature Little Bluestem is a native, warm-season, perennial mid-grass with bunch-forming habit. It grows from May until frost and grows to about one meter tall.

Flowers Spikelets are formed along numerous racemes up to 10 cm long. The spikelets are borne in pairs, one sessile and fertile, one pedicelled and sterile. Up to 200 flower stalks may be in a bunch.

Leaves In early growth the leaves are 3-8 mm wide, flattened at their base. Where the blades join the sheath is a narrow, whitish transverse line. Older leaves are folded.

Use or Importance Little Bluestem is a palatable and nutritious range grass and decreases under heavy grazing. This species is popular in prairie restorations and native plant gardens.

Habitat Often a conspicuous dominant in uplands; in moister situations it occurs as intermingled plants amongst the taller grasses. It has a much branched fibrous root system which penetrates to depths of 1-1/2 meters. It grows in dry, sandy or rocky soil.

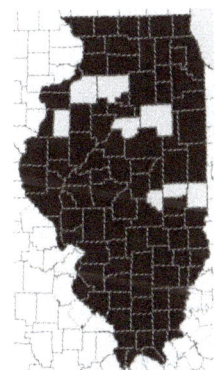
Distribution in Illinois

Distribution in central USA

Group F. Leaves long and narrow, with parallel veins. Flowers inconspicuous, green or brown or straw-colored, without petals.

INDIAN GRASS
Sorghastrum nutans (L.) Nash

INDIAN GRASS

Sorghastrum nutans (L.) Nash Literally, a "poor imitation of *Sorghum*", referring to its similarity to *Sorghum*.

Family Poaceae, or Grass Family

Season and Stature This native, warm-season perennial grass is a co-dominant, loosely tufted prairie grass with Big Bluestem. It attains heights between 1.5 to 2.0 or even 2.5 meters. Growth begins at about the same time as Big Bluestem (early May). Flowering is during late July and August.

Flowers The flowers are yellowish, due to the conspicuous, exserted, yellow anthers. The spikelets are borne in pairs, one sessile and perfect, the other reduced to a hairy pedicel. Spikelets are borne on short racemes which branch from the rachis in panicle-like fashion. Fertile spikelets terminate in a bent awn which is about four times the length of the fruit itself.

Leaves In its young growth, Indian Grass somewhat resembles Big Bluestem. Its leaves depart the stem (culm) at about a 45-degree angle. The blade, about 1.5 cm wide, noticeably narrows or tapers where it joins the culm. At the juncture of leaf and culm is a notched ligule about 2 to 3 mm long.

Use or Importance Indian Grass is a palatable grass for grazing or as a component of prairie hay. It is nutritious and sought out by grazing animals, but will decrease under heavy grazing. The seeds can be harvested by combine and are often used in restoration projects.

Habitat Tallgrass prairie. May invade drier uplands, especially where there has been some mild disturbance such as an occasional burning.

Distribution in Illinois

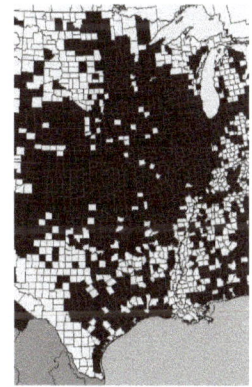
Distribution in central USA

Group F. Leaves long and narrow, with parallel veins. Flowers inconspicuous, green or brown or straw-colored, without petals.

TALL DROPSEED
Sporobolus compositus (Poir.) Merr.

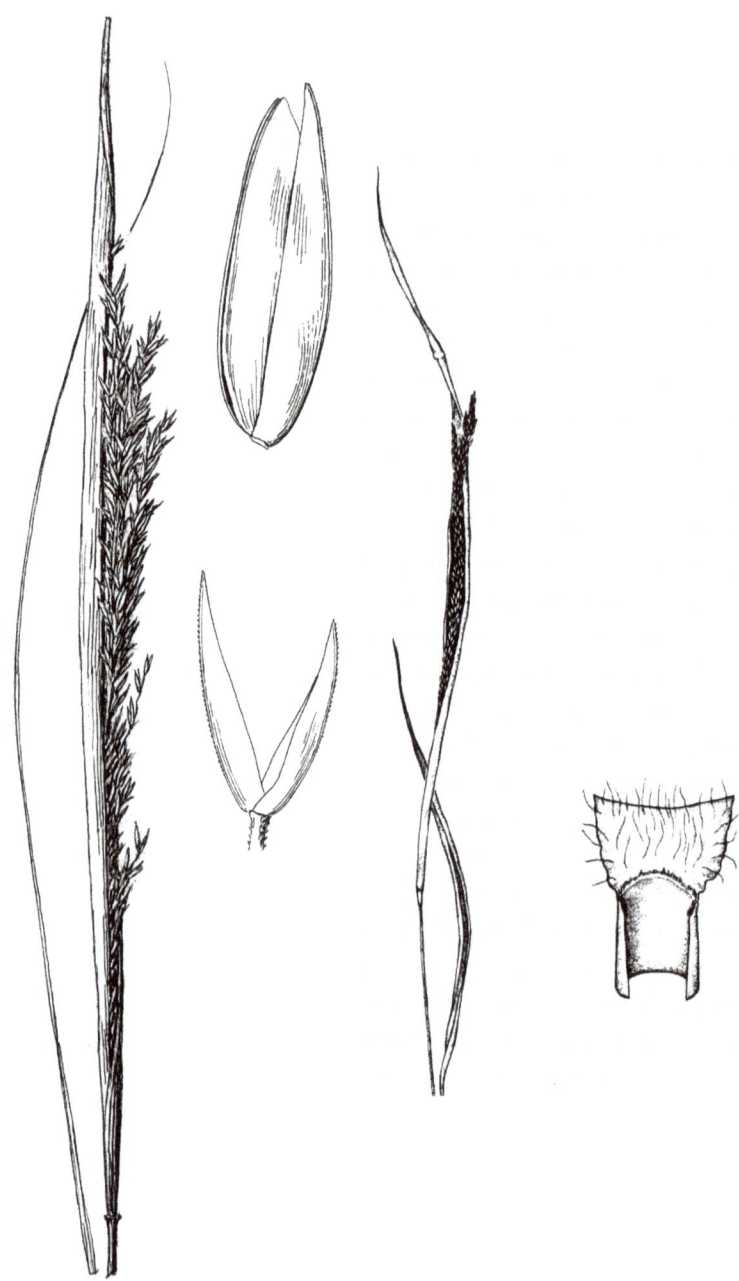

TALL DROPSEED

Sporobolus compositus (Poir.) Merr.

From the Greek *sporos* (seed) and *bolos* (throwing), referring to the ripe seed being easily released.

Synonym *Sporobolus asper* (Beauv.) Kunth

Family Poaceae, or Grass Family

Season and Stature Tall Dropseed is a native, warm-season perennial which has short rhizomes and tends to grow locally in pure stands. It grows to about one metertall. It flowers and produces its fruits in late Summer or early Fall.

Flowers A narrow panicle is enclosed by an inflated sheath. Typically, only one-third to one-half of the inflorescence emerges, and the fruits fall freely from the glumes, hence the name "dropseed."

Leaves The leaves of Tall Dropseed are long, narrow, and tapering. They tend to have about 1/4 of their length appearing dead or dry at the tips when mature. The leaf sheaths are hairy at the throat and the leaves are somewhat hairy at their base. The leaves bleach to a light color in winter.

Use or Importance Tall Dropseed is known as a hard grass because of its high proportion of fibers. It is not as palatable as the bluestems and behaves as an increaser for a time, since it is not a preferred choice by the grazing animal.

Habitat Slopes and level upland areas where the ground is packed or hard. Because it often forms nearly pure stands, it is suspected of allelopathic properties (that is, secreting compounds into the soil which restrict the establishment of other species).

Note Most common and widespread in Mixed Prairie, where it is well adapted to the drier conditions. Also successful in True Prairie in drier, open areas.

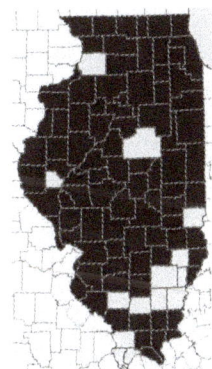

Distribution in Illinois

Distribution in central USA

Group F. Leaves long and narrow, with parallel veins. Flowers inconspicuous, green or brown or straw-colored, without petals.

SAND DROPSEED
Sporobolus cryptandrus (Torr.) Gray

SAND DROPSEED

Sporobolus cryptandrus (Torr.) Gray

From the Greek *sporos* (seed) and *bolos* (throwing), referring to the ripe seed being easily released.

Family Poaceae, or Grass Family

Season and Stature This native, warm-season perennial forms clumps because it has short rhizomes. The plant matures and flowers in late Summer. It grows to a height of 60 cm or more. It is a minor or secondary species of grass in True Prairie.

Flowers The panicle is open and is therefore different from the Tall Dropseed whose inflorescence scarcely emerges from the sheath. However, before maturity, Sand Dropseed also has its inflorescence mostly enclosed in the sheath. The spikelets are single-flowered and fall freely at maturity.

Leaves Recognition of Sand Dropseed is aided in vegetative condition because of the presence of copious white hairs radiating in all directions at the nodal areas.

Use or Importance Palatability is high in Sand Dropseed before it matures. After maturity, the plant is high in fiber and becomes a "hard" grass. The plant is considered somewhat of an invader in True Prairie.

Habitat As the name implies, the plant is well adapted to sandy soils. Sand Dropseed is also drought-tolerant, and increases during such periods.

 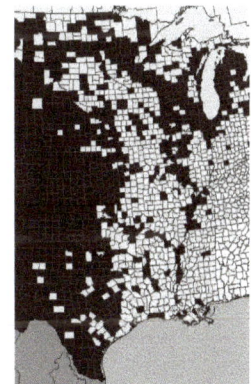

Distribution in Illinois *Distribution in central USA*

Group F. Leaves long and narrow, with parallel veins. Flowers inconspicuous, green or brown or straw-colored, without petals.

PRAIRIE DROPSEED
Sporobolus heterolepis (Gray) Gray

PRAIRIE DROPSEED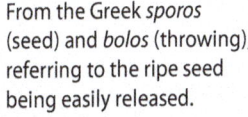

Sporobolus heterolepis (Gray) Gray

Family Poaceae, or Grass Family

From the Greek *sporos* (seed) and *bolos* (throwing), referring to the ripe seed being easily released.

Season and Stature Prairie Dropseed is a native, warm-season perennial which reaches a height of about one meter at flowering time. It is a mid-grass and flowers during the Fall.

Flowers The inflorescence is a well-developed panicle. Before flowering maturity, the inflorescence is held within the sheath. The spikelets are single-flowered and soon fall from the inflorescence.

Leaves The leaves of Prairie Dropseed are long and attenuated. The leaf length is often 60 cm or more. The final 1/3 of the leaf tends to become dry. The plant has a bunch habit, with the bunches having a diameter at their base of about 15 to 20 cm.

Use or Importance Prairie Dropseed is a palatable species and decreases under heavy grazing.

Habitat Prairie Dropseed grows on the uplands and may forms a community in which it is a dominant, sometimes forming from 50 to 80 per cent of the composition. It grows in dry, often sandy soil.

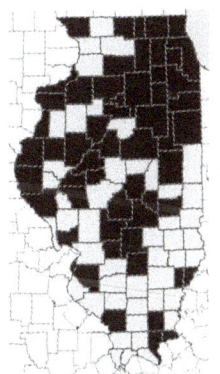

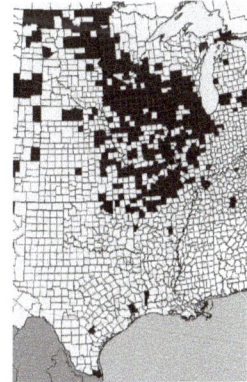

Distribution in Illinois   *Distribution in central USA*

Group F. Leaves long and narrow, with parallel veins. Flowers inconspicuous, green or brown or straw-colored, without petals.

PRAIRIE CORDGRASS
Sporobolus michauxianus (A.S. Hitch.) Peterson & Saarela

PRAIRIE CORDGRASS

Sporobolus michauxianus (A.S. Hitch.) Peterson & Saarela

Synonym *Spartina pectinata* Bosc ex Link

Family Poaceae, or Grass Family

From the Greek *sporos* (seed) and *bolos* (throwing), referring to the ripe seed being easily released.

Season and Stature Growing in the wettest part of the prairie is Prairie Cordgrass, a warm-season, sod-forming perennial which reaches heights up to 2 meters at flowering time. Ecologists place Prairie Cordgrass as a member of the last stage in the succession of the hydrosere. It flowers during the early Fall.

Flowers Paniculate inflorescences bear up to six or more short spikes, which have all the spikelets on one side of the panicle branches. The spikes are up to 6 cm long.

Leaves Leaves are 1 cm or more wide, up to 80 cm long, and have a prominent midvein. Leaves are light green in color, finely serrated at the margins, and tapered gradually throughout their length. The leaves must be handled with care or fingers or hands can be cut.

Use or Importance Prairie Cordgrass is grazed early in the season (if practicable due to the often wet conditions at that time). In late season, this grass becomes unpalatable. Cordgrass is valuable for the protection of waterways and for erosion control.

Habitat Favors low, wet, poorly aerated soils, and may grow where water stands a few inches deep in the Spring. These wet meadows may dry to the point where they are mowed for hay in the Summer.

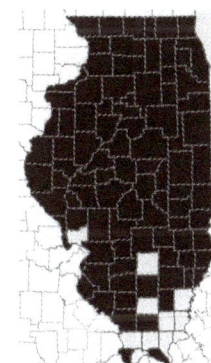 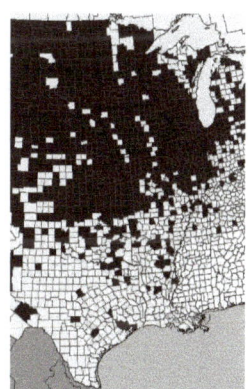

Distribution in Illinois   Distribution in central USA

Group F. Leaves long and narrow, with parallel veins. Flowers inconspicuous, green or brown or straw-colored, without petals.

EASTERN GAMA GRASS
Tripsacum dactyloides L.

EASTERN GAMA GRASS
Tripsacum dactyloides L.

Family Poaceae, or Grass Family

Season and Stature Eastern Gama Grass is a species of minor importance in our prairies due to its limited occurrence in Illinois (becoming more common south and west of the state). It is a native, warm-season perennial which grows in large bunches. The rhizomes are nearly as thick as one's finger. The plant may attain a height of up to 3 meters at flowering time (July and August).

Flowers The inflorescence is made up of 1 to 3 spikes bearing the staminate flowers above and the pistillate flowers below. These spikes are 15 to 25 cm long. The fruits are embedded or sunken in the rachis of the lower 1/3 or 1/4 of the spike. These break into individual pieces at maturity.

Leaves The leaves are long and up to 3.5 cm wide, tapering, and extremely sharp along their edges.

Use or Importance Eastern Gama Grass is palatable when grazed when young. With age, it becomes harsh and unpalatable. Gama Grass is possibly one of the remote ancestors of corn.

Habitat In the moisture gradient, Eastern Gama Grass grows where it is very moist. It will often be bordered on one side by Prairie Cordgrass, and on the drier side by Switch Grass. It sometimes is found growing with Big Bluestem.

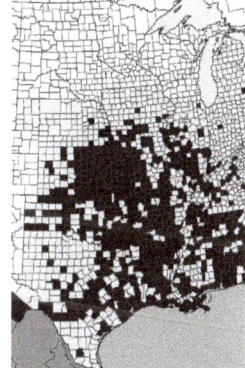

Distribution in Illinois   *Distribution in central USA*

Group F. Leaves long and narrow, with parallel veins. Flowers inconspicuous, green or brown or straw-colored, without petals.

SIX-WEEKS FESCUE
Vulpia octoflora (Walt.) Rydb.

SIX-WEEKS FESCUE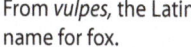
Vulpia octoflora (Walt.) Rydb.

From *vulpes*, the Latin name for fox.

Synonym *Festuca octoflora* Walt.

Family Poaceae, or Grass Family

Season and Stature The prairie grass flora is made up of few annual species, and Six-Weeks Fescue is a native annual, which grows and flowers during the cool-season, or during the early Summer. It forms tufts and grows to a height of about 15 cm. Its name is taken from its period of growth: it passes from seed germination to maturity in approximately six weeks.

Flowers The narrow panicle has four to ten spikelets, and several florets per spikelet. The entire plant turns brown or straw-colored at maturity and becomes easily recognized.

Leaves Erect, narrow.

Use or Importance Of little importance to grazing animals.

Habitat This small plant grows on a variety of soils and is usually found where the prairie has been thinned to a very open condition by overgrazing or other types of disturbance. It is an invading species in degenerating prairies.

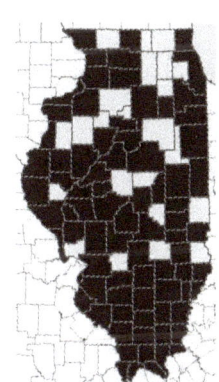
Distribution in Illinois

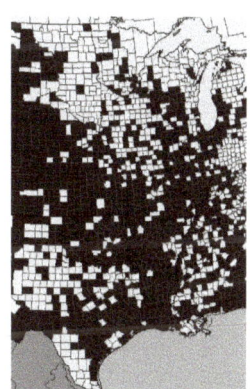
Distribution in central USA

Group F. Leaves long and narrow, with parallel veins. Flowers inconspicuous, green or brown or straw-colored, without petals.

PRAIRIE ROOTS

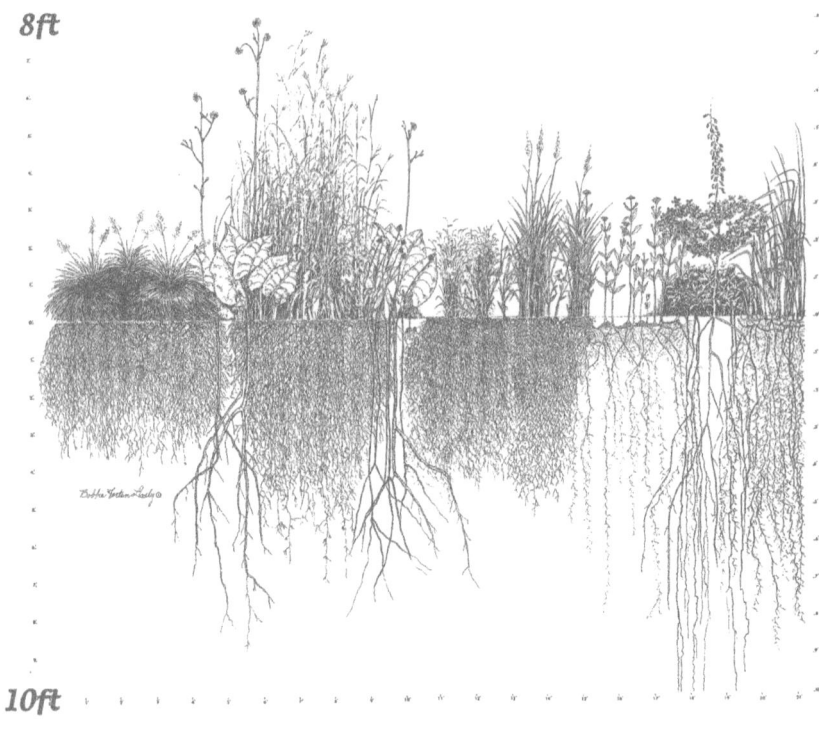

In the prairie, a large proportion of the biomass is actually underground in the form of roots (both fibrous and tap-roots), rhizomes, and tubers.

ACKNOWLEDGMENTS

For the 2019 edition:

Steve Chadde would like to give a grateful nod of appreciation to the original authors of *Prairie Plants of Illinois:* John Voigt and Robert Mohlenbrock, for their many contributions towards a better understanding and conservation of the natural heritage of Illinois. I hope that this edition of the book, revised and updated to reflect the latest nomenclatural and other changes, further contributes to that end. Additional thanks are due to photographers Joshua Mayer and Matt Lavin who provided many of the photographs used in this book (their excellent work can be seen on Flickr (*www.flickr.com*).

From the 1985 edition:

The authors are indebted to Dr. David Kenney, former Director of the Illinois Department of Conservation, to Mr. Allan Mickelson, State Forester, and to staff foresters Ernest Kunze, Dick Thorn and John Sester for their willingness to let us write about the prairie plants of Illinois. Thanks are also given to all our colleagues who helped us in any way in the preparation of this book.

We wish to thank Mr. Vernon Sternberg and the Southern Illinois University Press who were kind enough to let us use the following illustrations from the *Illustrated Flora of Illinois* series: *Andropogon gerardii, Bouteloua curtipendula, Dichanthelium oligosanthes, Hordeum pusillum, Iris virginica, Juncus tenuis, Juncus torreyi, Panicum capillare, Panicum virgatum, Poa pratensis, Schizachyrium scoparium, Sisyrinchium angustifolium, Sorghastrum nutans, Sporobolus compositus, Sporobolus cryptandrus, Sporobolus heterolepis, Sporobolus michauxianus,* and *Tripsacum dactyloides.*

We are grateful to Mr. Paul Nelson who did the illustration of *Salix humilis* and to Mr. Dan Malkovich and *Illinois Magazine* who let us use some material from that publication.

Thanks are also given to Mrs. Beverly Mohlenbrock who typed the manuscript.

REFERENCES

Listed below are a few non-technical field guides describing and illustrating prairie plants of the Midwest region.

Christiansen, Paul, and Mark Müller. 1999. *An Illustrated Guide to Iowa Prairie Plants*. University of Iowa Press. Iowa City, IA. 237 p.

Cochrane, Theodore S., Kandis Elliot, and Claudia S. Lipke. 2006. *Prairie Plants of the University of Wisconsin–Madison Arboretum*. University of Wisconsin Press. Madison, WI. 365 p.

Denison, Edgar. 1998. *Missouri Wildflowers*. Missouri Department of Conservation, Jefferson City, MO. 276 p.

Ladd, Doug, and Frank Oberle. 2005. *Tallgrass Prairie Wildflowers*. Falcon Press. Helena, MT. 272 p.

Mohlenbrock, R.H. 1986. *Guide to the Vascular Flora of Illinois*. Southern Illinois University Press, Carbondale, IL.

Müller, Mark. 2000. *Prairie in Your Pocket: A Guide to Plants of the Tallgrass Prairie*. Bur Oak guide, University of Iowa Press. Iowa City, IA.

Newcomb, Lawrence. 1977. *Newcomb's Wildflower Guide*. Little, Brown and Company. Boston, MA. 490 p.

Peterson, Roger Tory, and Margaret McKenny. 1968. *Peterson Field Guides, Wildflowers: Northeastern/Northcentral North America*. Houghton Mifflin Co. New York, NY. 420 p.

Runkel, Sylvan T., and Dean M. Roosa. 1999. *Wildflowers and Other Plants of Iowa Wetlands*. University of Iowa Press. Iowa City, IA. 388 p.

Thieret, John W., revising author. 2001. *The Audubon Society Field Guide to Wildflowers: Eastern Region*. Alfred A. Knopf, Inc. New York, NY. 879 p.

Vance, F.R., J.R. Jowsey, J.S. McLean, and F.A. Switzer. 1999. *Wildflowers of the Northern Great Plains*. University of Minnesota Press. Minneapolis, MN. 336 p.

INDEX

Synonyms are listed in italics.

Acerates viridiflora, 101
Alumroot, 39
American Feverfew, 189
American Germander, 139
American Vetch, 89
Amorpha canescens, 51
Andropogon
    gerardii, 239
    scoparius, 267
Anemone
    canadensis, 53
    caroliniana, 55
    patens, 81
Antennaria neglecta, 145
Arnoglossum plantagineum, 147
Aromatic Aster, 207
Arrow-Leaved Violet, 45
Artemisia ludoviciana, 149
Asclepias
    hirtella, 95, 151
    sullivantii, 97
    tuberosa, 153
    verticillata, 99
    viridiflora, 101, 155
Aster
    azureus, 209
    ericoides, 201
    laevis, 203
    novae-angliae, 205
    oblongifolius, 207
    sericeus, 211

Baptisia
    alba, 57
    bracteata, 59
    leucantha, 57
    leucophaea, 59

Big Bluestem, 239
Blue Hearts, 103
Blue Violet, 47
Bouteloua curtipendula, 241
Brickellia eupatorioides, 157
Brown-Eyed Susan, 191
Buchnera americana, 103
Bush Lespedeza, 71
Butterfly Weed, 153

Cacalia tuberosa, 147
Callirhoe triangulata, 159
Camassia scilloides, 215
Canadian Anemone, 53
Carex
    meadii, 243
    pensylvanica, 245
Carolina Anemone, 55
Carolina Rose, 85
Cassia fasciculata, 61
Ceanothus americanus, 161
Chamaecrista fasciculata, 61
Cicuta maculata, 63
Closed Gentian, 109
Clustered Poppy Mallow, 159
Comandra
    richardsiana, 163
    umbellata, 163
Common Spiderwort, 235
Common Sundrops, 185
Compass Plant, 195
Coneflower, Drooping, 83
Coreopsis palmata, 105
Culver's-Root, 141
Cup-Plant, 137

INDEX

Dalea
    candida, 65
    purpurea, 67
Dichanthelium oligosanthes, 247
Dodecatheon meadia, 35
Downy Gentian, 111
Drooping Coneflower, 83

Eastern Gama Grass, 279
Echinacea pallida, 165
Elymus canadensis, 248
Eryngium yuccifolium, 217
Euphorbia corollata, 167
Euthamnia graminifolia, 169

False Boneset, 157
False Sunflower, 121
False Toadflax, 163
Festuca octoflora, 281
Flat-Topped Spurge, 167
Fragaria virginiana, 37
Fringed Loosestrife, 123

Galium tinctorium, 107
Gentiana
    andrewsii, 109
    puberulenta, 111
Geum triflorum, 69
Goat's-Rue, 87
Golden Alexanders, 91
Grass-Leaved Goldenrod, 169
Green Milkweed, 101
Green Milkweed, 155

Hairy Green Milkweed, 95, 151
Hairy Sunflower, 115
Heath Aster, 201

Helianthus
    grosseserratus, 113, 171
    mollis, 115
    pauciflorus, 116
    pauciflorus, 117
    rigidus, 117
    tuberosus, 119, 173
Heliopsis helianthoides, 121
Hesperostipa spartea, 251
Heuchera richardsonii, 39
Hoary Puccoon, 181
Hordeum pusillum, 253
Hypoxis hirsuta, 219

Indian Grass, 269
Indian Plantain, 147
Iris
    brevicaulis, 221
    shrevii, 223
    virginica, 223

Jerusalem Artichoke, 119, 173
Juncus
    tenuis, 255
    torreyi, 257
June Grass, 259

Kentucky Bluegrass, 265
Koeleria
    cristata, 259
    macrantha, 259
Kuhnia eupatorioides, 157

Leadplant, 51
Lespedeza
    capitata, 71
    virginica, 73

INDEX

Liatris
    aspera, 175
    pycnostachya, 177
    squarrosa, 179
Lilium
    michiganense, 225
    philadelphicum, 227
Lithospermum canescens, 181
Little Bluestem, 267
Little Wild Barley, 253
Lobelia spicata, 183
Lysimachia ciliata, 123

Mead's Sedge, 243
Monarda fistulosa, 125
Mountain Mint, 129

Narrow-Leaved Blue-Eyed Grass, 229
Needlegrass, 251
New England Aster, 205
New Jersey Tea, 161
Nodding Wild Rye, 249

Oenothera pilosella, 185
Orbexilum pedunculatum, 75

Packera paupercula, 187
Pale Prairie Coneflower, 165
Panicum
    capillare, 261
    oligosanthes, 247
    virgatum, 263
Parthenium integrifolium, 189
Partridge Pea, 61
Pasque-Flower, 81
Path Rush, 255

Pediomelum tenuiflorum, 77
Pennsylvania Sedge, 245
Petalostemum
    candidus, 65
    purpureus, 67
Phlox pilosa, 127
Poa pratensis, 265
Polytaenia nuttallii, 79
Prairie Cordgrass, 277
Prairie Dock, 41
Prairie Dropseed, 275
Prairie Groundsel, 187
Prairie Hyssop, 131
Prairie Parsley, 79
Prairie Phlox, 127
Prairie Sage, 149
Prairie Spiderwort, 231
Prairie Violet, 43
Prairie Willow, 193
Prairie-Smoke, 69
Primula meadia, 35
Psoralea
    psoralioides, 75
    tenuiflora, 77
Pulsatilla patens, 81
Purple Prairie Clover, 67
Pussy-Toes, 145
Pycnanthemum
    tenuifolium, 129
    virginianum, 131

Ratibida pinnata, 83
Rattlesnake Master, 217
Rosa carolina, 85
Rosinweed, 135
Rough Blazing-Star, 175
Rough Heuchera, 39

INDEX

Rudbeckia hirta, 191
Ruellia humilis, 133

Salix humilis, 193
Sampson's Snakeroot, 75
Sand Dropseed, 273
Sawtooth Sunflower, 113, 171
Scaly Blazing-star, 179
Schizachyrium scoparium, 267
Scribner's Panic Grass, 247
Scurf Pea, 77
Senecio pauperculus, 187
Shooting-star, 35
Side-Oats Grama, 241
Silky Aster, 211
Silphium
    integrifolium, 135
    laciniatum, 195
    perfoliatum, 137
    terebinthinaceum, 41
Sisyrinchium angustifolium, 229
Six-Weeks Fescue, 281
Sky-Blue Aster, 209
Smooth Aster, 203
Solidago
    canadensis, 197
    graminifolia, 169
    rigida, 199
Sorghastrum nutans, 269
Spartina pectinata, 277
Spiderwort, 233
Spiked Lobelia, 183
Sporobolus
    asper, 271
    compositus, 271
    cryptandrus, 273
    heterolepis, 275
    michauxianus, 277

Stiff Goldenrod, 199
Stiff Marsh Bedstraw, 107
Stiff Sunflower, 117
Stiff Tickseed, 105
Stipa spartea, 251
Sullivant's Milkweed, 97
Switchgrass, 263
Symphyotrichum
    ericoides, 201
    laeve, 203
    novae-angliae, 205
    oblongifolium, 207
    oolentangiense, 209
    sericeum, 211

Tall Dropseed, 271
Tall Gayfeather, 177
Tall Goldenrod, 197
Tephrosia virginiana, 87
Teucrium canadense, 139
Torrey's Rush, 257
Tradescantia
    bracteata, 231
    ohiensis, 233
    virginiana, 235
Tripsacum dactyloides, 279
Turk's-Cap Lily, 225

Veronicastrum virginicum, 141
Vicia americana, 89
Viola
    pedatifida, 43
    sagittata, 45
    sororia, 47
Virginia Blue Flag, 223
Virginia Lespedeza, 73
Vulpia octoflora, 281

INDEX

Water Hemlock, 63
Western Lily, 227
White False Indigo, 57
White Prairie Clover, 65
Whorled Milkweed, 99
Wild Bergamot, 125
Wild False Indigo, 59
Wild Hyacinth, 215
Wild Petunia, 133
Wild Strawberry, 37
Witch Grass, 261

Yellow Star-Grass, 219

Zigzag Iris, 221
Zizia aurea, 91

www.ingramcontent.com/pod-product-compliance
Lightning Source LLC
Chambersburg PA
CBHW040221040426
42333CB00049B/3028